The Convenience Foods Cookbook

Quick & Healthy Recipes Based on Brand-name Foods

Nancy Cooper, RD, LD, CDE

IDC Publishing

MINNEAPOLIS

IDC Publishing
3800 Park Nicollet Boulevard
Minneapolis, Minnesota 55416-2699
(612) 993-3393
www.idcpublishing.com

Library of Congress Cataloging-in-Publications Data

Cooper, Nancy, R.D.
The convenience foods cookbook: quick & healthy recipes based on brand-name foods/ Nancy Cooper.

     p.   cm.

Includes index.
ISBN 1-885115-46-6
1. Cookery. 2. Convenience foods. 3. Brand name products – United States. I. Title.
TX652.C745   1998
641.5 – dc21   98-12638
                                            CIP

Printed in the United States of America

Publisher: Karol Carstensen
Production Manager: Gail Devery
Associate Editor: Sara Frueh
Cover and Text Design: MacLean & Tuminelly

Table of Contents

Acknowledgments

I would like to thank several individuals for their help in completing this book. First, a special thank you to the many food companies who provided us with recipes using their convenience foods. Without their willingness to share this information, this book would not have been possible. Second, to the IDC Publishing staff, Karol Carstensen, Sara Frueh, and Gail Devery, who provided creativity, organization, direction and support in countless ways during the development and production of this book.

I would also like to thank Shirley Upham for her excellent typing skills; dietetic intern Sarah Galanis and Shannon Perron, RD, for assistance with the nutrition analysis of the recipes; and the entire staff of the International Diabetes Center, especially the dietitians, for their encouragement and innovative ideas on using convenience foods. I also must thank my family who is always willing to "taste test" recipes and provide honest feedback with a smile.

Lastly, I am grateful to the readers of this book. I hope this cookbook will be a valuable resource as you strive to combine convenience in the kitchen with good taste and nutrition.

Introduction

As our lives have become increasingly busy and our time more valuable, food manufacturers and supermarkets have obliged our demand for quick and easy meal solutions with many new convenience food products. From simple frozen side dishes to complete meal kits in a box, it's possible to find almost everything nearly ready-to-eat in the aisles of the supermarket.

The purpose of this cookbook is to help you expand your thinking about convenience foods and how you use them. Not only are they the entree or side dish they're intended to be; they're also handy, wholesome ingredients for quick home-cooked meals. Just think of convenience foods as simple shortcuts you can take on the way to dishes that are truly your own.

The recipes in this book were chosen for their innovative, nutritious use of convenience foods. Many were developed and tested in the kitchens of food manufacturers; some we've modified slightly to improve the nutritional value. Also, the central ingredient or ingredients in all the recipes are true convenience foods that are substantial enough to help you save time in the kitchen and tasty enough to help you save face at the table. On your busiest days, look for recipes with this symbol: ☻. They can be prepared in less than 20 minutes!

We hope this book bridges the gap between convenience and creativity, between your need for speed and your desire for good taste. In addition to the many great recipes throughout the book, on the next few pages you'll find tips for adding nutritional balance and flavor to convenience food meals and recipes, as well as convenience food ideas for speeding up the preparation time of any recipe.

Convenience *and* Nutrition

Historically, convenience foods, such as soup starters, pasta salad mixes and frozen entrees, have had a well-earned reputation for being loaded with fat, calories, salt and other additives. While this is still true of some convenience foods, anyone who has visited a supermarket lately knows it's no longer the whole story. Reduced-calorie, low-fat and low-salt products are readily available, as are convenience foods made from only vegetarian or organic ingredients.

If you choose carefully, convenience foods can be as healthy and nutritious as any dish you make in your own kitchen. For low-fat choices, look for convenience foods that meet the following guidelines.

Food Category	Low-fat Guideline
Frozen meals and entrees, and other foods that make up most of a meal	3 grams of fat or less per 100 calories, and no more than $1/3$ of total fat from saturated fat
Cheese	5 grams of fat or less per serving
Side dishes, snacks, cereals, and other foods	3 grams of fat or less per serving

A potential pitfall of even the healthiest convenience food meals is a lack of nutritional variety and balance. You may find a tasty, healthful version of frozen spaghetti and meatballs, for example, but that alone is not going to fulfill the requirements of a well-balanced meal.

You can bump up the nutrition quotient of convenience foods by adding foods from the missing food groups. Add a salad (from a bag!) to your spaghetti dinner or top a frozen pizza with fresh or frozen vegetables. Boxed rice or pasta mixes can benefit from the addition of diced cooked chicken breast and a vegetable side dish to create a complete meal.

Preparation Tips for Low-fat Convenience

The way you prepare convenience foods can influence their nutritional value, too. It's not always necessary to follow the package directions exactly; substituting or even deleting some ingredients can lower the fat or sodium content without compromising quality or taste. This also is true for many of your favorite scratch recipes. All you need is the courage to experiment!

- Skip or reduce the butter or margarine called for in boxed rice and pasta side dishes. This lowers fat content and barely affects flavor.
- Use reduced-fat cheese, sour cream, cream cheese and other dairy products. In recipes that call for cream or whole milk, use evaporated skim milk instead.
- Use nonstick cooking pans to fry or sauté foods, and coat with vegetable cooking spray instead of oil to prevent sticking.
- Choose canned vegetables – such as roasted peppers and artichoke hearts – that are packed in water instead of oil.
- Choose water-packed tuna or salmon instead of fish canned in oil.
- In recipes, use 2 egg whites in place of 1 whole egg, or use an egg substitute, to lower fat and cholesterol.
- Use extra-lean ground beef and other lean cuts of meat, and trim visible fat before cooking. Drain and rinse cooked ground meat before adding to recipes.

- Choose poultry that's skinned prior to packaging, or remove the skin before cooking poultry or using it in recipes.
- Sauté vegetables in broth or water instead of oil.
- Try using only half the contents of seasoning packets packaged with soup, pasta and rice mixes to cut down on sodium.
- Rinse canned vegetables under running water and cook in fresh water to reduce sodium content.

Adding Flavor and Flair

Food companies design most convenience foods to appeal to a wide range of consumers, and that usually means playing it safe with spices. If you prefer zesty fare, you may need to put on your chef's hat and do it yourself. Fortunately, this doesn't take a lot of time – a few sprinkles of dried herbs or ground spices can enliven a dish in seconds. Start with $\frac{1}{4}$ to $\frac{1}{2}$ teaspoon of dried herbs or spices for a four-serving dish, and add more if needed. (The flavor in 1 tablespoon of fresh herbs is about equal to 1 teaspoon of dried herbs.)

To add flavor to ...	use ...
Beans, baked	Cloves, ginger, molasses, brown sugar, mustard, ketchup, honey, onion
Chili, canned or mix	Chiles, cumin, chili powder, cayenne pepper, cilantro, onion, green pepper
East Asian foods	Ginger, coriander, cilantro, sesame oil, tamari, chili paste, mint, lemongrass, cumin, fish sauce
Fish fillets, frozen	Dill, fennel, parsley, thyme, lemon juice
Indian foods	Curries (spice blends), cayenne pepper, coriander, cloves, cumin, turmeric, cinnamon
Italian foods	Oregano, basil, garlic, sage, rosemary, fennel
Macaroni and cheese	Pepper, paprika, tomatoes, onion
Mexican foods	Cumin, chiles, cilantro, cinnamon
Middle Eastern foods	Mint, coriander, rosemary, marjoram, nutmeg, cumin, saffron
Pasta sauce, jar	Oregano, basil, parsley, garlic, crushed red pepper, green or red pepper, mushrooms, olives, onion
Pasta side dishes	Basil, oregano, garlic, ricotta cheese, Parmesan or Romano cheese

To add flavor to ...	use ...
Pizza, frozen	Chopped fresh vegetables, green or black olives, chile peppers, oregano, basil, fennel, crushed red pepper, minced garlic
Potatoes, scalloped or au gratin	Dill, cilantro, chives, saffron, tarragon, basil, garlic, tomatoes, corn, onion
Rice side dishes	Rosemary, thyme, chives, parsley, garlic, onion
Soup, broth	Bay leaf, parsley, pasta or noodles, rice, chopped vegetables
Soup, cream or cheese	Chives, thyme, sage, nutmeg, parsley
Soup, tomato	Basil, oregano, sage, saffron, rice, onion
Stew	Basil, chili powder, oregano, bay leaf, thyme, allspice, dry sherry
Stuffing mix	Rosemary, sage, thyme, apples, raisins, cranberries, celery, apricots, nuts

Time-saving Substitutions

Are some of your favorite recipes sitting unused in a recipe box or cookbook, shelved because of lack of time? Dust them off and take another look – incorporating convenience-food ingredients can slash preparation time and make those recipes realistic daily options.

If your recipe calls for ...	use ...
Bacon, crumbled	Bacon bits in a jar
Chicken breast, fresh	Frozen boneless, skinless chicken-breast fillets
Cooked turkey, chicken, ham	Pre-cooked deli meats, canned chunk chicken, or frozen cooked, cubed chicken breast
Fruit, fresh-cut	Frozen fresh fruit or fresh-cut fruit from the deli
Garlic, chopped	Chopped garlic in a jar or garlic powder
Glaze for meat or vegetables	Jam, jelly, pourable fruit, honey, bottled sauces or glazes
Gravy	Dry gravy mix or gravy in a jar
Green pepper, chopped	Frozen chopped green pepper
Herbs, fresh	Dried herbs or chopped herbs packed in water in a jar
Lettuce or fresh salad greens	Salad mix in a bag

If your recipe calls for ...	use ...
Mashed or shredded potatoes	Dry mashed potato mix or frozen or refrigerated mashed or shredded potatoes
Mushrooms, sliced	Canned mushrooms or pre-sliced fresh mushrooms
Onion, chopped	Frozen chopped onion
Pie crust	Frozen or refrigerated pie crust or dry pie crust mix
Pizza crust	Refrigerated pizza crust, dry pizza crust mix, foccacia, or bread shells
Roasted red peppers	Roasted red peppers in a jar
Shrimp, fresh cooked	Frozen or canned cooked shrimp
Tomatoes, chopped	Canned diced tomatoes

About the Nutrition Information in This Book

Nutrition information per serving is provided for each recipe in this book and includes calories, total fat, saturated fat, protein, carbohydrate, sodium, fiber, exchanges, and carbohydrate choices. The nutrition data were calculated using the Nutrition Data System from the University of Minnesota Nutrition Coordinating Center.

If an ingredient amount is listed as a range – for example, 1 to 2 teaspoons of sugar – the nutrient analysis is based on the first (smallest) amount listed. Optional ingredients, including "salt and pepper to taste," are not included in the analysis, and all nutrition data are rounded to the nearest whole number.

Food Exchanges

The nutrition data in this book includes exchange information for each recipe. This information is essential for people who follow a meal plan based on the food exchange system, including people trying to control their weight and people with health conditions such as diabetes or heart disease.

To use the exchange system, you need an individualized meal plan that tells you how many servings or exchanges you should select from each exchange list for meals and snacks. If you would like more information about meal planning and the exchange system, contact a registered dietitian. To locate a registered dietitian in your area, ask your doctor, call your local hospital or public health department, or call The American Dietetic Association's Nutrition Hotline at 1-800-366-1655.

Carbohydrate Choices

To help people who want to count carbohydrates, the number of carbohydrate choices per serving is included for each recipe in this book. Carbohydrate counting is a method of food planning used by people with diabetes to help keep blood glucose (sugar) levels from going too high or too low. Carbohydrate is a nutrient found in grains and starchy vegetables, fruits and fruit juices, and milk and milk products. It is the main nutrient in food that raises blood glucose levels.

Carbohydrate choices are calculated using the "15-Gram Equation." This states that 1 carbohydrate choice is the amount of a food that contains about 15 grams of carbohydrate. If you are familiar with the exchange lists, think of 1 carbohydrate choice as equal to 1 serving from the starch, fruit or milk list.

You can determine the number of carbohydrate choices provided by most food products from the Nutrition Facts label. For example, if the label states that a ½ cup serving of pasta sauce contains 15 grams of carbohydrate, you'd count 1 serving of sauce as 1 carbohydrate choice. If you use 1 cup of sauce, however, you'd count the portion as 2 carbohydrate choices (30 grams of carbohydrate).

Of course, the number of grams of carbohydrate in foods is not always neatly divisible by 15, and carbohydrate counting is not an exact science. The simple chart below helps solve this problem by converting carbohydrate grams to carbohydrate choices for you.

Carbohydrate Grams	Carbohydrate Choices
0–5	0
6–10	½
11–20	1
21–25	1½
26–35	2
36–40	2½
41–50	3
51–55	3½
56–65	4
66–70	4½
71–80	5

If you have diabetes, carbohydrate counting is a great way to add flexibility and variety to your diet. You can learn more about carbohydrate counting from a registered dietitian. (See page ix for information about locating a dietitian in your area.)

Appetizers and Snacks

Chili Party Dip ◔

1 can (15 ounces) Hormel® Turkey Chili No Beans
1 package (8 ounces) fat-free cream cheese
1 jar (4 ounces) Chi-Chi's® Diced Green Chilies
¼ cup finely chopped fresh or frozen onion
4 drops hot pepper sauce

1. In saucepan, combine chili, cream cheese, chilies, onion and hot pepper sauce.
2. Heat on medium until cheese melts, stirring frequently.
3. Serve with chips or cubed bread.

Serves: 14   Serving size: ¼ cup

NUTRITION FACTS PER SERVING

Calories	70	*Carbohydrate choices*	0
Carbohydrate	4 g		
Protein	5 g	*Exchanges*	1 meat
Fat	4 g		
Saturated fat	2 g		
Fiber	<1 g		
Sodium	295 mg		

Extra Special Spinach Dip ☉

1 envelope Lipton® Recipe Secrets® Vegetable Soup Mix
1 container (16 ounces) light or nonfat sour cream
½ cup light mayonnaise
½ teaspoon lemon juice
1 package (10 ounces) frozen chopped spinach, thawed and squeezed dry
1 can (8 ounces) water chestnuts, drained and chopped

1. In medium bowl, blend vegetable soup mix, sour cream, mayonnaise and lemon juice.
2. Stir in spinach and water chestnuts; chill until served. Serve with chips, bread cubes or cut-up fresh vegetables.

Serves: 24   Serving Size: 2 tablespoons

Variations

Stir in 2 tablespoons chopped green onion, radishes or crumbled blue cheese; or omit water chestnuts and add 1 cup chopped apple.

NUTRITION FACTS PER SERVING

Calories	52	*Carbohydrate choices*	0
Carbohydrate	5 g		
Protein	2 g	*Exchanges*	I vegetable
Fat	3 g		½ fat
Saturated fat	I g		
Fiber	I g		
Sodium	210 mg		

Double Bean Dip

1 envelope Lipton® Recipe Secrets® Savory Herb with Garlic or Golden Onion Soup Mix
1 can (16 ounces) chickpeas or garbanzo beans, rinsed and drained
1 can (16 ounces) cannelini or white kidney beans, rinsed and drained
¼ cup olive or vegetable oil
1 tablespoon finely chopped fresh parsley or 1 teaspoon dried parsley
2 teaspoons lemon juice
¼ teaspoon ground black pepper

1. In food processor or mixing bowl, combine all ingredients until almost smooth.
2. Cover and chill at least 2 hours.

Serves: 24   Serving size: 2 tablespoons

Serving Suggestion

Serve with pita bread cut into triangles, bread sticks, snow peas, carrot sticks or assorted crackers.

NUTRITION FACTS PER SERVING

Calories 61
Carbohydrate 7 g
Protein 2 g
Fat 3 g
Saturated fat <1 g
Fiber 2 g
Sodium 240 mg

Carbohydrate choices ½

Exchanges ½ starch
½ fat

Hidden Valley® Bacon & Cheddar Dip ○

1 packet (1 ounce) Hidden Valley® Original Ranch® Party Dip
2 cups light sour cream
¼ cup bacon bits
1 cup shredded reduced-fat cheddar cheese

1. Combine party dip and sour cream in medium bowl.
2. Add bacon bits and cheese.
3. Mix well and refrigerate until served.

Serves: 26   Serving size: 2 tablespoons

NUTRITION FACTS PER SERVING

Calories	45	*Carbohydrate choices*	0
Carbohydrate	2 g		
Protein	2 g	*Exchanges*	1 fat
Fat	3 g		
Saturated fat	1 g		
Fiber	<1 g		
Sodium	191 mg		

Lipton® Recipe Secrets® Dip Recipes ⓒ

1 envelope Lipton® Recipe Secrets® Beef Onion, Golden Onion, Onion, Onion-Mushroom, Vegetable, Savory Herb with Garlic, Italian Herb with Tomato or Golden Herb with Lemon Soup Mix
1 container (16 ounces) light or nonfat sour cream

1. In small bowl, blend soup mix with sour cream.
2. Cover and chill.

Serves: 16   Serving size: 2 tablespoons

Serving Suggestions

Stir in bacon bits, shredded carrots or chopped radishes. Serve with bread sticks, toasted pita bread wedges, crackers or assorted fresh vegetables, such as celery or carrot sticks, green pepper strips or cherry tomatoes.

NUTRITION FACTS PER SERVING

Calories	66	*Carbohydrate choices*	½
Carbohydrate	8 g		
Protein	3 g	*Exchanges*	½ starch
Fat	3 g		½ fat
Saturated fat	1 g		
Fiber	1 g		
Sodium	369 mg		

Original Crispix® Mix

7 cups Kellogg's® Crispix® cereal
1 cup mixed nuts
1 cup pretzels
3 tablespoons margarine, melted
¼ teaspoon garlic salt
¼ teaspoon onion salt
2 teaspoons lemon juice
4 teaspoons Worcestershire sauce

Oven Directions

1. Preheat oven to 250° F. Combine cereal, nuts and pretzels in a 13 x 9 x 2-inch baking pan. Set aside.
2. In small mixing bowl, stir together remaining ingredients and add to cereal mixture, gently stirring until evenly coated.
3. Bake about 45 minutes, stirring every 15 minutes. Spread on paper towels to cool. Store in airtight container.

Microwave Directions

1. In large microwave-safe bowl, combine cereal, nuts and pretzels.
2. In small mixing bowl, stir together remaining ingredients and add to cereal mixture, gently stirring until evenly coated.
3. Microwave on high 4 minutes, stirring after 2 minutes. Spread on paper towels to cool. Store in airtight container.

Serves: 18   Serving size: ½ cup

NUTRITION FACTS PER SERVING

Calories	118	*Carbohydrate choices*	1
Carbohydrate	13 g		
Protein	2 g	*Exchanges*	1 starch
Fat	7 g		1 fat
Saturated fat	1 g		
Fiber	1 g		
Sodium	275 mg		

Spinach Rice Balls

1½ cups cooked rice
1 package (10 ounces) frozen chopped spinach, cooked and well-drained
½ cup (about 2 ounces) shredded mozzarella cheese
⅓ cup plain dry bread crumbs
2 eggs, slightly beaten
¼ cup grated Parmesan cheese
¼ cup skim milk
1 teaspoon Dijon-style or brown prepared mustard
1 envelope Lipton® Recipe Secrets® Golden Onion Soup Mix
Vegetable cooking spray
Assorted mustards for dipping, optional

1. Preheat oven to 375° F. In medium bowl, combine cooked rice, spinach, mozzarella cheese, bread crumbs, eggs, Parmesan cheese, milk, mustard and soup mix. Mix well.
2. Shape into 1-inch balls. Arrange on baking sheet sprayed with cooking spray.
3. Bake 20 minutes or until golden. Serve warm with assorted mustards, if desired.

Serves: 8   Serving size: 3 balls

NUTRITION FACTS PER SERVING

Calories	128	*Carbohydrate choices*	1
Carbohydrate	16 g		
Protein	7 g	*Exchanges*	1 starch
Fat	4 g		1 lean meat
Saturated fat	2 g		
Fiber	2 g		
Sodium	718 mg		

Golden Chicken Nuggets ☉

1 envelope Lipton® Recipe Secrets® Onion-Mushroom Soup Mix
¾ cup plain dry bread crumbs
1¼ pounds boneless, skinless chicken breast, cut into 1-inch pieces
Vegetable cooking spray
3 tablespoons margarine or butter, melted

1. Preheat oven to 400° F. In medium mixing bowl, combine soup mix and bread crumbs.
2. Dip chicken pieces in bread crumb mixture, coating well.
3. Spray a 13 x 9-inch baking or roasting pan with cooking spray and arrange chicken in single layer. Drizzle with margarine.
4. Bake 10 minutes or until chicken is done, turning once.

Serves: 6   Serving size: 4 nuggets

Variations

For Cajun style chicken nuggets, add 1½ teaspoons chili powder, 1 teaspoon ground cumin and ¼ teaspoon ground red pepper to bread crumb mixture. Use Lipton® Recipe Secrets® Onion, Golden Onion or Savory Herb with Garlic Soup Mix in place of Onion-Mushroom Soup Mix.

NUTRITION FACTS PER SERVING

Calories	234	*Carbohydrate choices*	1
Carbohydrate	13 g		
Protein	23 g	*Exchanges*	1 starch
Fat	9 g		3 lean meat
Saturated fat	2 g		
Fiber	1 g		
Sodium	822 mg		

Mini Mexican Meatballs

1 envelope Lipton® Recipe Secrets® Onion or Beefy Onion Soup Mix
1½ pounds extra-lean ground beef
1 egg
1 tablespoon cornmeal, optional
1 jar (4 ounces) Chi-Chi's® Diced Green Chilies, undrained, divided
1 can (14½ ounces) whole peeled tomatoes, undrained and chopped
1 teaspoon ground cumin, optional
Baked tortilla chips, optional

1. In medium bowl, combine soup mix, ground beef, egg, cornmeal and
   1 tablespoon chilies; shape into 1-inch meatballs.
2. In 12-inch skillet, brown meatballs over medium-high heat; drain.
3. Add tomatoes, remaining chilies and cumin, if desired. Bring to a boil
   over high heat; cook 1 minute.
4. Reduce heat to low and simmer, covered, 8 minutes or until meatballs
   are done. Serve with tortilla chips, if desired.

Serves: 16   Serving size: 3 meatballs

NUTRITION FACTS PER SERVING

Calories	97	*Carbohydrate choices*	0
Carbohydrate	3 g		
Protein	9 g	*Exchanges*	1 meat
Fat	5 g		
Saturated fat	2 g		
Fiber	<1 g		
Sodium	346 mg		

Quick BBQ Appetizer Meatballs

1 package (11 ounces) Morningstar Farms® Prime Patties
1 bottle (18 ounces) barbecue sauce
2 tablespoons lemon juice

1. Defrost patties in refrigerator overnight or at room temperature for 1 hour.
2. Preheat oven to 350° F. Divide and shape each burger patty into 8 small, round balls by rolling between palms of both hands. Place meatballs on baking sheet and bake for 15 minutes.
3. Combine barbecue sauce and lemon juice in medium sauce pan over low heat. Place baked meatballs in warm sauce. Transfer to chafing dish and keep warm.

Serves: 8   Serving size: 4 meatballs

NUTRITION FACTS PER SERVING

Calories	104	*Carbohydrate choices*	1
Carbohydrate	11 g		
Protein	11 g	*Exchanges*	1 starch
Fat	2 g		1 very lean meat
Saturated fat	<1 g		
Fiber	2 g		
Sodium	671 mg		

Easy Italian Turnovers

1 envelope Lipton® Recipe Secrets® Italian Herb with Tomato Soup Mix
1 pound extra-lean ground beef
¾ cup chopped onion
½ cup water
½ cup bread crumbs
2 tablespoons grated Parmesan cheese
1 package (15 ounces) refrigerated pie crust for 2 crusts (9 inches each)
Vegetable cooking spray

1. Preheat oven to 350° F. In medium bowl, combine all ingredients except pie crust; set aside.
2. Open pie crusts; cut each into quarters to make 8 quarters. Place ¼ cup beef mixture on 1 side of each quarter crust. Fold crust in half over mixture so that long edges meet and seal edges using fork.
3. Arrange turnovers on baking sheet sprayed with cooking spray and bake 25 minutes or until pastry is golden brown.

Serves: 8   Serving size: 1 turnover

Variations

Substitute Lipton® Recipe Secrets® Savory Herb with Garlic or Onion-Mushroom Soup Mix.

NUTRITION FACTS PER SERVING

Calories	435	*Carbohydrate choices*	2
Carbohydrate	35 g		
Protein	17 g	*Exchanges*	2 starch
Fat	25 g		2 meat
Saturated fat	7 g		3 fat
Fiber	2 g		
Sodium	890 mg		

Antipasto Pizza

1 (16-ounce) Italian bread shell or foccacia
½ cup Land O Lakes® Light Sour Cream
¼ teaspoon garlic powder
2 cups (¾ pound) deli antipasto salad, drained and coarsely chopped
3 tablespoons chopped fresh parsley, optional

1. Preheat oven to 450° F. Place bread shell on baking sheet.
2. In small bowl, stir together sour cream and garlic powder; spread evenly over bread shell to within ½ inch of edge.
3. Top with chopped salad and parsley, if desired. Bake for 20 to 22 minutes or until heated through and golden brown. Cut into 8 slices.

Serves: 8   Serving size: ⅛ pizza (1 slice)

Variation

For Vegetable Shrimp Pizza, replace antipasto salad with ¾ pound deli marinated vegetables, chopped and drained, 1 cup (4 ounces) Land O Lakes® Shredded Cheddar Cheese and 3 ounces cooked salad shrimp.

NUTRITION FACTS PER SERVING

Calories	229	*Carbohydrate choices*	2
Carbohydrate	30 g		
Protein	8 g	*Exchanges*	2 starch
Fat	9 g		1 ½ fat
Saturated fat	3 g		
Fiber	1 g		
Sodium	643 mg		

Chopped Pizza

8 Rhodes Texas Rolls™, thawed
1 cup diced cooked ham
4 tablespoons chopped green onions
1 cup (4 ounces) shredded reduced-fat cheddar cheese
1 cup (4 ounces) shredded part-skim mozzarella cheese
Vegetable cooking spray

1. Preheat oven to 350° F. Thaw rolls until soft (about 2 hours at room temperature).
2. Place 2 rolls on lightly floured bread board. Top with ¼ cup ham, 1 tablespoon green onions and ¼ cup each of cheddar and mozzarella cheeses. Chop with a knife until ingredients are evenly mixed into rolls. Lift dough mixture with a spatula onto baking sheet that has been sprayed with cooking spray.
3. Repeat same procedure with remaining 6 rolls, using 2 rolls at a time. Shape each dough mixture into a 6-inch pizza.
4. Cover with plastic wrap that has also been sprayed with cooking spray and allow to rise 20 to 30 minutes. Remove wrap.
5. Bake for 20 to 25 minutes or until golden brown. Place baking sheet on a wire rack to cool. Cut each pizza into 6 wedges.

Serves: 12   Serving size: 2 wedges

NUTRITION FACTS PER SERVING

Calories 173
Carbohydrate 19 g
Protein 11 g
Fat 6 g
Saturated fat 2 g
Fiber 1 g
Sodium 414 mg

Carbohydrate choices 1

Exchanges 1 starch
1 meat

Bean and Cheese Pinwheels

¾ cup refried beans
4 (6-inch) flour tortillas
½ cup sliced green onions
8 slices Kraft® Mexican Style Singles Process Cheese Food
Salsa, optional

1. Spread 3 tablespoons beans on each tortilla.
2. Top each tortilla with 2 tablespoons onion and 2 slices cheese singles. Roll up tightly and wrap securely in plastic wrap.
3. Refrigerate 30 minutes. Cut each roll into 6 slices; secure with toothpicks. Serve with salsa, if desired.

Serves: 8   Serving size: 3 spirals

NUTRITION FACTS PER SERVING

Calories	115	*Carbohydrate choices*	1
Carbohydrate	11 g		
Protein	6 g	*Exchanges*	1 starch
Fat	6 g		1 fat
Saturated fat	3 g		
Fiber	2 g		
Sodium	329 mg		

Ham & Cheese Tortilla Melts ◑

1 package (10) Buena Vida™ Fat Free Flour Tortillas
1 cup (4 ounces) shredded reduced-fat cheddar cheese
3 tablespoons sliced green onions
10 slices (1 ounce each) lean ham
Mustard, optional
Vegetable cooking spray

1. Divide cheese and onion evenly between tortillas. Place on tortillas to within ½ inch of edges.
2. Arrange ham slices on top of cheese and onions. Top with mustard, if desired. Fold bottom half of tortilla over ham slice to form a half moon shape.
3. Heat a large nonstick skillet that has been lightly coated with cooking spray. Cook tortillas over medium heat until golden brown and cheese is melted; turn with a spatula and brown the other side. Serve immediately.

Serves: 10   Serving size: 1 tortilla

NUTRITION FACTS PER SERVING

Calories	160	*Carbohydrate choices*	1
Carbohydrate	14 g		
Protein	12 g	*Exchanges*	1 starch
Fat	6 g		1 meat
Saturated fat	2 g		
Fiber	1 g		
Sodium	599 mg		

Chicken Quesadillas ☺

1 can (10¾ ounces) Campbell's® Healthy Request® Condensed Cream of
   Chicken Soup
1 teaspoon chili powder
½ cup shredded reduced-fat cheddar cheese
2 cans (5 ounces each) Swanson® Premium Chunk White Chicken, drained
8 (8-inch) flour tortillas
Water

1. Preheat oven to 400° F. Combine soup, chili powder, cheese and
   chicken in medium bowl.
2. Place tortillas on 2 baking sheets. Top half of each tortilla with about
   ¼ cup soup mixture. Spread to within ½ inch of edges.
3. Moisten edges of tortillas with water; fold over and press edges
   together. Bake for 10 minutes or until hot.

Serves: 8   Serving size: 1 quesadilla

NUTRITION FACTS PER SERVING

Calories	234	*Carbohydrate choices*	2
Carbohydrate	27 g		
Protein	13 g	*Exchanges*	2 starch
Fat	7 g		1 meat
Saturated fat	2 g		
Fiber	1 g		
Sodium	545 mg		

Hot Chili Cheese Triangles

1 package (10) Buena Vida™ Fat Free Flour Tortillas
1 container (12 ounces) fat-free cream cheese, softened
1 can (15 ounces) Hormel® Turkey Chili with Beans
1½ cups shredded reduced-fat cheddar cheese

1. Preheat oven to 375° F. Remove tortillas from refrigerator; let stand at room temperature for at least 15 minutes.
2. Spread each tortilla with about 2 tablespoons cream cheese. Spread 1 heaping tablespoon chili over cream cheese.
3. Sprinkle 1 to 2 tablespoons shredded cheese over chili. Gently fold tortilla in half to form a half moon shape. Press edges lightly with fingers to seal.
4. Wrap individually in aluminum foil with all edges of foil sealed. Bake 10 minutes or until heated through and cheese is melted. To serve, cut each tortilla into 4 wedges.

Serves: 10   Serving size: 4 wedges

NUTRITION FACTS PER SERVING

Calories	213	*Carbohydrate choices*	1½
Carbohydrate	21 g		
Protein	15 g	Exchanges	1½ starch
Fat	8 g		2 lean meat
Saturated fat	3 g		
Fiber	2 g		
Sodium	574 g		

Cheesy Apple and Ham Sandwich ⊙

½ *English muffin, toasted*
1 slice Kraft® Free® Cheddar Singles Nonfat Process Cheese Product
3 slices Oscar Mayer® Free Fat Free Deli-thin Honey Baked Cooked Ham
2 slices apple
1 tablespoon plain nonfat yogurt
Ground cinnamon

1. Layer muffin half with cheese slice, ham and apple slices.
2. Top with yogurt and sprinkle lightly with cinnamon.

Serves: 1   Serving size: 1 sandwich

NUTRITION FACTS PER SERVING

Calories	163	*Carbohydrate choices*	1½
Carbohydrate	21 g		
Protein	14 g	*Exchanges*	1½ starch
Fat	2 g		1 very lean meat
Saturated fat	<1 g		
Fiber	2 g		
Sodium	815 mg		

Nacho Nachos ☺

1 can (16 ounces) Old El Paso® Fat Free Refried Beans
¾ cup Old El Paso® Salsa
8 ounces low-fat baked tortilla chips
8 ounces (2 cups) shredded reduced-fat cheddar cheese
Old El Paso® Pickled Jalapeño Slices, optional

Microwave Directions

1. Combine refried beans and salsa; mix well.
2. Arrange half of tortilla chips in a single layer on large microwave-safe platter.
3. Spread half of the bean mixture on chips. Top with 1 cup cheese and jalapeño slices, if desired.
4. Microwave on high for 1½ to 3½ minutes or until cheese is melted.
5. Layer remaining ingredients on top, in same order. Repeat step 4.

Serves: 8   Serving size: ⅛ recipe

NUTRITION FACTS PER SERVING

Calories	238	*Carbohydrate choices*	2
Carbohydrate	33 g		
Protein	13 g	*Exchanges*	2 starch
Fat	6 g		1 meat
Saturated fat	3 g		
Fiber	5 g		
Sodium	509 mg		

Black Bean Salsa ☺

1 can (15 ounces) Eden® Black Beans, drained
½ cup chunky-style salsa

1. Mix beans and salsa together and serve with tortilla chips or warm tortillas.

Serves: 4   Serving size: ½ cup

NUTRITION FACTS PER SERVING

Calories	138
Carbohydrate	26 g
Protein	8 g
Fat	<1 g
Saturated fat	<1 g
Fiber	7 g
Sodium	302 mg

Carbohydrate choices 2

Exchanges 1 starch
             1 very lean meat

Taco Bites ⏲

¼ cup Kellogg's® Corn Flakes Crumbs
1 package (1¼ ounces) taco seasoning mix
2 tablespoons grated Parmesan cheese
1 package (13.2 ounces) Kellogg's® Eggo Mini's® Waffles, slightly toasted
Vegetable cooking spray
Salsa, optional
Light sour cream, optional

1. Preheat oven to 375° F. In large zipper bag, combine corn flakes crumbs, taco seasoning mix and Parmesan cheese. Set aside.
2. Break toasted waffles apart. Spray each side with cooking spray. Place waffles in bag with taco seasoning mixture. Gently shake to coat each waffle.
3. Heat a large nonstick skillet that has been lightly coated with cooking spray. Heat waffles about 10 minutes or until they are crisp. May be served with warm salsa and light sour cream, if desired.

Serves: 12   Serving size: 4 pieces

NUTRITION FACTS PER SERVING

Calories	107	*Carbohydrate choices*	1
Carbohydrate	16 g		
Protein	3 g	*Exchanges*	1 starch
Fat	4 g		½ fat
Saturated fat	1 g		
Fiber	1 g		
Sodium	346 mg		

Baked Vegetable & Seafood Wontons

1 envelope Lipton® Recipe Secrets® Vegetable Soup Mix
1 container (15 ounces) light ricotta cheese
½ pound imitation crabmeat, chopped, or 1½ cups cooked shrimp, chopped
¼ teaspoon garlic powder
⅛ teaspoon ground black pepper
40 refrigerated or frozen wonton wrappers, thawed
Water
Vegetable cooking spray
1 tablespoon olive or vegetable oil

1. Preheat oven to 350° F. In medium bowl, combine vegetable soup mix, cheese, crabmeat, garlic powder and pepper.
2. Place 1 tablespoon mixture on center of each wonton wrapper. Brush edges with water; fold each corner into center and press to seal.
3. Arrange seam-side-down on baking sheet lightly sprayed with cooking spray. Brush wontons with oil.
4. Bake 25 minutes or until crisp and golden brown, turning once.

Serves: 20   Serving size: 2 wontons

Tip

Cover unbaked wontons with a damp cloth until ready to bake; brush with oil just before baking.

NUTRITION FACTS PER SERVING

Calories	96	*Carbohydrate choices*	I
Carbohydrate	12 g		
Protein	6 g	*Exchanges*	I starch
Fat	3 g		I very lean meat
Saturated fat	I g		
Fiber	<I g		
Sodium	309 mg		

Soups and Stews

25

Chicken Gumbo ⏱

3 tablespoons vegetable oil
1 pound boneless, skinless chicken breast, cut into 1-inch pieces
½ pound smoked sausage, cut into ¾-inch slices
1 bag (16 ounces) frozen Birds Eye® Farm Fresh Mixtures Broccoli, Corn
   and Red Peppers
1 can (14½ ounces) stewed tomatoes
1½ cups water

1. Heat oil in large saucepan over high heat. Add chicken and sausage;
   cook until browned, about 8 minutes.
2. Add vegetables, tomatoes and water; bring to a boil. Reduce heat to
   medium; cover and cook 3 minutes. Serve hot.

Serves: 10   Serving size: 1 cup

NUTRITION FACTS PER SERVING

Calories	192	*Carbohydrate choices*	1
Carbohydrate	12 g		
Protein	15 g	*Exchanges*	½ starch
Fat	10 g		1 vegetable
Saturated fat	2 g		2 meat
Fiber	1 g		
Sodium	453 mg		

Chicken Enchilada Soup

1 tablespoon vegetable oil
¼ cup chopped onion
1 clove garlic, minced
¾ cup Country Sides™ Sweet 'n' Hot Pepper and Onion Relish
1½ cups chicken broth
½ cup evaporated skim milk
1 cup diced cooked chicken breast
¾ cup reduced-fat Monterey Jack cheese

1. Heat oil in large saucepan over medium heat. Add onion and garlic and sauté until tender.
2. Add relish and chicken broth and simmer, covered, for 15 minutes over low heat.
3. Add evaporated skim milk and chicken. Simmer another 8 to 10 minutes on low heat.
4. Stir in cheese, and serve hot.

Serves: 4   Serving size: about 1 cup

NUTRITION FACTS PER SERVING

Calories	249	*Carbohydrate choices*	1½
Carbohydrate	22 g		
Protein	21 g	*Exchanges*	1½ starch
Fat	9 g		2 lean meat
Saturated fat	3 g		
Fiber	1 g		
Sodium	928 mg		

Arizona Chicken Chili ☺

3 boneless, skinless chicken breasts, diced
1 can (14½ ounces) Del Monte® FreshCut™ Diced Tomatoes with Green
 Pepper and Onion
1 tablespoon chili powder
1 can (15¼ ounces) black beans or kidney beans, drained
1 can (15¼ ounces) Del Monte® FreshCut™ Golden Sweet Whole Kernel
 Corn, drained
¼ cup chopped cilantro or sliced green onions
Shredded Monterey Jack cheese, diced avocado, sliced radishes, or chopped
 green onions for garnish, optional

1. Combine chicken, tomatoes and chili powder in medium saucepan.
   Cook over medium heat about 5 minutes or until chicken is done and
   sauce is slightly thickened.
2. Add remaining ingredients, except garnishes, and simmer 5 to 7 minutes
   or until heated through.
3. Top with garnishes, if desired.

Serves: 6   Serving size: 1 cup

NUTRITION FACTS PER SERVING

Calories	248	*Carbohydrate choices*	2½
Carbohydrate	37 g		
Protein	21 g	*Exchanges*	2 starch
Fat	3 g		1 vegetable
Saturated fat	1 g		2 very lean meat
Fiber	7 g		
Sodium	628 mg		

Chicken 'N Dumplings Soup ◔

1 can (10¾ ounces) 98% fat-free condensed cream of chicken soup
3 cups water
2 cups cooked diced or shredded skinless chicken breast
6 Buena Vida® Fat Free Flour Tortillas
Salt and pepper to taste, optional

1. In large sauce pan, mix together soup and water. Bring to a boil; add chicken.
2. Tear or cut tortillas into pieces and add to boiling soup. Reduce heat and cook over medium-low heat for 8 to 10 minutes, stirring occasionally.
3. Season to taste with salt and pepper, if desired. Serve hot.

Serves: 10   Serving size: 1 cup

NUTRITION FACTS PER SERVING

Calories	113	*Carbohydrate choices*	½
Carbohydrate	10 g		
Protein	10 g	*Exchanges*	½ starch
Fat	3 g		1 lean meat
Saturated fat	1 g		
Fiber	<1 g		
Sodium	325 mg		

Turkey Chowder ☾

1 bag (20 ounces) frozen vegetables for soup
2 cups water
¼ teaspoon dried thyme leaves
⅛ teaspoon salt
Dash pepper
1 jar (12 ounces) Heinz® Fat Free Turkey Gravy
2 cups cubed cooked turkey

1. In large saucepan, combine vegetables, water, thyme, salt and pepper. Cover; bring to a boil. Simmer 8 minutes until vegetables are crisp-tender.
2. Stir in gravy and turkey; heat through and serve hot.

Serves: 8   Serving size: 1 cup

NUTRITION FACTS PER SERVING

Calories	110	*Carbohydrate choices*	1
Carbohydrate	11 g		
Protein	13 g	*Exchanges*	½ starch
Fat	2 g		1 vegetable
Saturated fat	<1 g		1 lean meat
Fiber	4 g		
Sodium	178 mg		

Southwestern Corn Chowder ☺

½ pound cooked ham, cut into ½-inch cubes
1 can (16½ ounces) cream-style corn
1 can (11 ounces) whole kernel corn with green and red peppers, drained
1 can (4 ounces) chopped green chiles
1 cup Land O Lakes® Light Sour Cream
1 cup skim milk

1. In 4-quart saucepan combine ham, cream-style corn, corn and chiles. Cook over medium high heat, stirring occasionally, until mixture just comes to a boil (2 to 3 minutes).
2. Reduce heat to low. Stir in sour cream and milk; continue cooking, stirring occasionally, until heated through (3 to 4 minutes).

Serves: 8   Serving size: 1 cup

NUTRITION FACTS PER SERVING

Calories	191	*Carbohydrate choices*	1½
Carbohydrate	24 g		
Protein	14 g	*Exchanges*	1½ starch
Fat	6 g		1 meat
Saturated fat	2 g		
Fiber	2 g		
Sodium	508 mg		

Tuscan Pasta and Bean Soup ☺

1 can (28 ounces) Contadina® Dalla Casa Buitoni Seasoned Crushed
*   Tomatoes with Roasted Garlic*
2 cans (13½ ounces each) beef broth
2 cans (15 ounces each) Great Northern or kidney beans, undrained
1 cup uncooked pasta shells
6 tablespoons grated Parmesan cheese

1. Combine crushed tomatoes, broth and beans with liquid in large saucepan; bring to a boil.
2. Add pasta; cook over medium heat for 10 to 12 minutes or until pasta is tender.
3. Sprinkle each serving with 1 tablespoon Parmesan cheese; serve hot.

Serves: 12   Serving size: 1 cup

NUTRITION FACTS PER SERVING

Calories	173	*Carbohydrate choices*	1½
Carbohydrate	30 g		
Protein	11 g	*Exchanges*	1½ starch
Fat	1 g		1 very lean meat
Saturated fat	<1 g		
Fiber	6 g		
Sodium	618 mg		

Quick and Easy Beef Stew

2 tablespoons cornstarch
2 tablespoons water
1 tablespoon vegetable oil
1 pound boneless beef sirloin steak, cut into 1-inch cubes
1 tablespoon chili powder
¾ cup Pace® Picante Sauce
1 can (15 ounces) black beans
1 can (15 ounces) pinto beans
1 can (14½ ounces) stewed tomatoes

1. In small bowl, mix cornstarch and water until smooth. Set aside.
2. Heat oil in Dutch oven over medium-high heat. Cook beef and chili powder until beef is browned, stirring often.
3. Add picante sauce, black beans, pinto beans and tomatoes. Heat to a boil. Cover and cook over low heat 5 minutes or until beef is done.
4. Add cornstarch mixture and stir. Cook until mixture boils and thickens, stirring constantly.

Serves: 9   Serving size: 1 cup

NUTRITION FACTS PER SERVING

Calories	228	*Carbohydrate choices*	2
Carbohydrate	31 g		
Protein	19 g	*Exchanges*	2 starch
Fat	4 g		2 very lean meat
Saturated fat	1 g		
Fiber	8 g		
Sodium	431 mg		

Alphabet Pizza Soup

Vegetable cooking spray
1 package (about 1¼ pounds) The Turkey Store® Lean Ground Turkey
1 can (14½ ounces) no-salt-added tomatoes, undrained and cut up
1 can (8 ounces) pizza sauce
3 cups water
2 cups frozen mixed vegetables
¼ cup uncooked alphabet macaroni
½ teaspoon garlic powder
½ teaspoon onion powder
½ teaspoon oregano
½ teaspoon salt, optional
8 tablespoons shredded part-skim mozzarella cheese

1. Spray large saucepan or Dutch oven with cooking spray. Heat over medium-high heat about 30 seconds. Crumble turkey into pan. Cook and stir 3 to 5 minutes or until turkey is lightly browned.
2. Add tomatoes, pizza sauce and water; mix well. Bring to a boil.
3. Add vegetables, macaroni, garlic powder, onion powder, oregano and salt, if desired.
4. Reduce heat to medium. Cook 10 to 15 minutes or until vegetables and pasta are tender, stirring frequently.
5. Sprinkle each serving with about 1 tablespoon cheese.

Serves: 8   Serving size: 1 cup

NUTRITION FACTS PER SERVING

Calories	190	*Carbohydrate choices* ½
Carbohydrate	9 g	
Protein	18 g	*Exchanges* ½ starch or 2 vegetable
Fat	9 g	2 meat
Saturated fat	3 g	
Fiber	2 g	
Sodium	221 mg	

Hearty Hamburger Soup

½ pound extra-lean ground beef
1 jar (12 ounces) Heinz® Fat Free Beef Gravy
1 can (14½ ounces) diced tomatoes
1⅓ cups water
1½ cups frozen mixed vegetables
⅓ cup uncooked small pasta shells or elbow macaroni
½ teaspoon dried basil
Salt and pepper to taste, optional
Shredded Parmesan cheese, optional

1. In medium saucepan, brown ground beef; drain.
2. Add gravy, tomatoes, water, frozen vegetables, pasta and basil. Simmer 15 minutes.
3. Season to taste with salt and pepper. Garnish with shredded Parmesan cheese, if desired.

Serves: 8   Serving size: 1½ cups

NUTRITION FACTS PER SERVING

Calories	149	*Carbohydrate choices*	1
Carbohydrate	15 g		
Protein	15 g	*Exchanges*	1 starch
Fat	4 g		2 very lean meat
Saturated fat	1 g		
Fiber	2 g		
Sodium	516 mg		

Salads

Greek Chicken Salad ☺

1 cup Kraft® Free® Italian Fat Free Dressing
1 teaspoon dried oregano leaves, crushed
1 pound boneless, skinless chicken breast, cut into strips
1 package (10 ounces) salad greens
1 package (4 ounces) Athenos® Crumbled Feta Cheese
3 plum tomatoes, sliced
½ cucumber, seeded, sliced and quartered
½ cup thinly sliced red onion
1 can (2¼ ounces) pitted ripe olives, drained

1. Mix dressing and oregano.
2. Heat 3 tablespoons of the dressing mixture in large skillet over medium heat.
3. Cook chicken in dressing mixture 8 minutes or until cooked through.
4. Toss greens, cheese, tomatoes, cucumber, red onion and olives with remaining dressing mixture. Place on serving platter.
5. Arrange chicken over greens mixture and serve.

Serves: 9   Serving size: 1½ cups

NUTRITION FACTS PER SERVING

Calories	182	*Carbohydrate choices*	½
Carbohydrate	9 g		
Protein	20 g	*Exchanges*	½ starch or 2 vegetable
Fat	7 g		2 lean meat
Saturated fat	4 g		
Fiber	2 g		
Sodium	736 mg		

Turkey Tortellini Salad

Vegetable cooking spray
1 package (about 1½ pounds) The Turkey Store® Boneless Breast Tenderloins
⅓ cup water
*1 package (6 ounces) tri-color cheese-filled tortellini pasta, cooked and
  cooled*
1 cup cherry tomatoes, halved
½ cup chopped green pepper
¼ cup sliced green onions
⅔ cup fat-free peppercorn ranch dressing
8 large lettuce leaves
¼ cup shredded carrot

1. Spray large skillet with cooking spray. Heat over medium-high heat
   about 30 seconds. Add turkey breast tenderloins. Brown on both sides.
2. Add water, and reduce heat to low. Cook, covered, 30 to 40 minutes or
   until no longer pink in center.
3. Remove turkey from skillet. Refrigerate until thoroughly cooled. Cut
   into ¾-inch cubes.
4. In large bowl, combine turkey, pasta, tomatoes, green pepper, onions
   and dressing.
5. Line large platter with lettuce leaves. Top with salad mixture and sprinkle with carrot. Serve cold.

Serves: 8   Serving size: ⅛ recipe

NUTRITION FACTS PER SERVING

Calories	177	*Carbohydrate choices*	1
Carbohydrate	12 g		
Protein	22 g	*Exchanges*	1 starch
Fat	4 g		3 very lean meat
Saturated fat	1 g		
Fiber	1 g		
Sodium	248 mg		

Tarragon Chicken Salad

4 boneless, skinless chicken-breast halves (about 1¼ pounds), cooked and
*   cubed; or 20 ounces frozen, cooked chicken, thawed and cubed*
1 cup red grapes, halved
¾ cup Miracle Whip® Light Salad Dressing
1 teaspoon dried tarragon leaves

1. Combine all ingredients. Refrigerate several hours or overnight.

Serves: 6   Serving size: ⅙ recipe

Serving Suggestion

Serve in lettuce-lined pita breads as a sandwich.

NUTRITION FACTS PER SERVING

Calories	206	*Carbohydrate choices*	1
Carbohydrate	11 g		
Protein	21 g	*Exchanges*	1 fruit
Fat	9 g		3 lean meat
Saturated fat	2 g		
Fiber	<1 g		
Sodium	288 mg		

Chicken Caesar Salad ⊙

1 tablespoon vegetable oil

4 boneless, skinless chicken-breast halves (about 1¼ pounds), slightly
flattened

1 bag (10 ounces) complete Caesar salad mix, prepared as directed

1. Heat oil in large nonstick skillet over medium-high heat. Add chicken-breast halves; sauté, turning over once, until browned and no longer pink in center, 8 to 10 minutes. Transfer chicken to platter and keep warm.
2. Divide salad on 4 serving plates.
3. Cut each chicken breast diagonally into ½-inch-thick strips, keeping strips of each breast piece together. Arrange 1 sliced chicken breast on top of each plate of lettuce.

Serves: 4   Serving size: ¼ recipe

NUTRITION FACTS PER SERVING

Calories	330	*Carbohydrate choices*	0
Carbohydrate	5 g		
Protein	34 g	*Exchanges*	1 vegetable
Fat	19 g		4 meat
Saturated fat	4 g		
Fiber	1 g		
Sodium	182 mg		

Lobster Spinach Salad ⊙

1 package (8 ounces) Louis Kemp® Lobster Delights®
1 package (10 ounces) pre-washed and cut spinach
1 can (4 ounces) sliced mushrooms, drained
4 ounces fat-free Italian dressing
4 tablespoons grated Parmesan cheese, optional

1. Combine all ingredients except Parmesan cheese.
2. Top each serving with 1 tablespoon Parmesan cheese, if desired.

Serves: 4   Serving size: ¼ recipe

NUTRITION FACTS PER SERVING

Calories	106	*Carbohydrate choices*	1
Carbohydrate	14 g		
Protein	10 g	*Exchanges*	½ starch
Fat	2 g		1 vegetable
Saturated fat	1 g		1 very lean meat
Fiber	3 g		
Sodium	922 mg		

Italian Tuna Salad Toss ☺

8 cups torn mixed salad greens
1 can (14 ounces) artichoke hearts, canned in water, drained and quartered
1 can (9¼ ounces) tuna in water, drained and flaked
½ pound fresh green beans, cooked and drained
1 cup sliced plum tomatoes
1 cup Kraft® Free® Italian Fat Free Dressing

1. Toss all ingredients to coat with dressing.

Serves: 7   Serving size: 2 cups

Variations

Substitute ½ pound sliced cooked turkey, chicken or roast beef, cut into strips, for tuna.

NUTRITION FACTS PER SERVING

Calories	106	*Carbohydrate choices*	1
Carbohydrate	14 g		
Protein	13 g	*Exchanges*	1 starch or 3 vegetable
Fat	<1 g		1 very lean meat
Saturated fat	<1 g		
Fiber	5 g		
Sodium	646 mg		

Seven Seas® Sensational Steak Salad

1 cup Seven Seas® Viva Light Italian Dressing, divided
1 pound flank steak
1 package (10 ounces) mixed salad greens
1 cup cherry tomatoes, halved
½ cup seasoned croutons

1. Pour ¾ cup dressing over steak; cover and refrigerate 30 minutes or longer to marinate. Drain; discard dressing.
2. Grill or broil steak until desired doneness. Cut into ¼-inch thick strips.
3. Toss steak with greens, tomatoes and remaining dressing; top with croutons.

Serves: 4   Serving size: ¼ recipe

NUTRITION FACTS PER SERVING

Calories	244	*Carbohydrate choices* ½	
Carbohydrate	8 g		
Protein	26 g	*Exchanges*	½ starch or 2 vegetable
Fat	12 g		3 lean meat
Saturated fat	4 g		½ fat
Fiber	2 g		
Sodium	203 mg		

Crunchy Bean and Cheese Salad

1 can (16 ounces) three-bean salad, drained
1 jar (7 ounces) roasted red peppers, drained and diced
4 ounces Muenster cheese, cut into ¹/₂-inch cubes
1 can (2.8 ounces) French's® French Fried Onions, divided
¹/₄ cup chopped green olives
¹/₄ cup chopped fresh Italian parsley
1 tablespoon olive oil
1 tablespoon balsamic vinegar

1. In large bowl, combine all ingredients except ¹/₃ cup onions.
2. Cover; refrigerate 30 minutes. Sprinkle with remaining ¹/₃ cup onions just before serving.

Serves: 10   Serving size: ¹/₂ cup

Tip

For warm, crispy onion flavor, microwave French Fried Onions on microwave-safe dish on high for 1 minute.

NUTRITION FACTS PER SERVING

Calories	198	*Carbohydrate choices*	¹/₂
Carbohydrate	9 g		
Protein	5 g	*Exchanges*	¹/₂ starch
Fat	17 g		3 fat
Saturated fat	4 g		
Fiber	2 g		
Sodium	441 mg		

Southwest Bean & Corn Salad ☉

½ cup Kraft® Free® Thousand Island Fat Free Dressing
¼ teaspoon black pepper
4 cups torn mixed salad greens
1 can (16 ounces) black beans, rinsed and drained
1 package (10 ounces) frozen corn, thawed and drained
½ cup chopped red pepper
½ cup thinly sliced red onion, optional

1. Mix dressing and black pepper. Set aside.
2. Divide and arrange greens onto 4 serving plates.
3. Mix beans, corn and red pepper. Top each plate of greens equally with the bean mixture.
4. Garnish with red onion, if desired. Serve with dressing mixture on the side.

Serves: 8   Serving size: 1 cup

NUTRITION FACTS PER SERVING

Calories	135	*Carbohydrate choices*	2
Carbohydrate	28 g		
Protein	6 g	*Exchanges*	2 starch
Fat	1 g		
Saturated fat	< 1 g		
Fiber	5 g		
Sodium	302 mg		

Light 'N Lean Vegetable Stir-fry Salad ☉

2 quarts water
1 bag (16 ounces) Flav-R-Pac® Vegetable Stir-Fry with Noodles®
1 cup cubed cooked chicken or turkey, or drained, water-packed tuna
½ cup bottled light salad dressing

1. Bring water to a boil in large saucepan. Add vegetable stir-fry with
   noodles. Once water returns to a boil, remove from heat, drain in
   colander and rinse under cold running water to cool.
2. Stir in meat and dressing. Refrigerate.

Serves: 4   Serving size: 1

Serving Suggestion

Serve as a sandwich in pita bread with shredded lettuce and shredded
cheese.

NUTRITION FACTS PER SERVING

Calories	168	*Carbohydrate choices*	1½
Carbohydrate	22 g		
Protein	14 g	*Exchanges*	1 starch
Fat	3 g		1 vegetable
Saturated fat	1 g		1 lean meat
Fiber	6 g		
Sodium	354 mg		

Dole® Pear and Cheese Salad ☺

1 package (10 ounces) Dole® European Special Blend Salad
½ cup Dole® Pitted Dates, sliced
3 tablespoons vegetable oil
3 tablespoons white wine vinegar
1 large Dole® pear, cored and thinly sliced
¼ cup crumbled gorgonzola or blue cheese
¼ cup chopped walnuts, toasted

1. Toss salad blend and dates in large bowl; set aside.
2. Combine oil and vinegar in small bowl. Pour over salad; toss to coat evenly.
3. Evenly divide salad onto 6 salad plates.
4. Arrange pear slices in a fan shape over each salad. Sprinkle with cheese and nuts.

Serves: 6   Serving size: ⅙ recipe

Tip
To toast walnuts, bake at 350° F, 10 to 12 minutes or until golden brown.

NUTRITION FACTS PER SERVING

Calories	134	*Carbohydrate choices*	1
Carbohydrate	20 g		
Protein	3 g	*Exchanges*	1 fruit
Fat	12 g		1 vegetable
Saturated fat	2 g		2 fat
Fiber	3 g		
Sodium	84 mg		

Carrot Pineapple Salad ◔

$\frac{1}{2}$ cup Miracle Whip® Light Salad Dressing
3 cups shredded carrots
1 can (8$\frac{1}{4}$ ounces) crushed pineapple tidbits, packed in juice, drained
$\frac{1}{2}$ cup raisins
1 tablespoon sugar

1. Combine all ingredients and refrigerate.

Serves: 5   Serving size: $\frac{1}{2}$ cup

Serving Suggestion

Place 2 tablespoons carrot pineapple salad on top of ham, chicken or turkey in a sandwich.

NUTRITION FACTS PER SERVING

Calories	87	*Carbohydrate choices*	1
Carbohydrate	17 g		
Protein	1 g	*Exchanges*	1 fruit
Fat	3 g		1 vegetable
Saturated fat	<1 g		$\frac{1}{2}$ fat
Fiber	1 g		
Sodium	109 mg		

Apple Slaw ☺

1 package (16 ounces) Dole® Coleslaw Mix
1 large diced apple
½ cup Miracle Whip® Light Salad Dressing
1 tablespoon sugar
Salt and pepper to taste, optional

1. Place coleslaw mix in large bowl. Add apple.
2. Combine dressing, sugar and salt and pepper, if desired. Stir into coleslaw mixture until blended. Refrigerate until serving.

Serves: 5   Serving size: ⅕ recipe

NUTRITION FACTS PER SERVING

Calories	121	*Carbohydrate choices*	1
Carbohydrate	19 g		
Protein	1 g	*Exchanges*	1 fruit
Fat	5 g		1 vegetable
Saturated fat	1 g		1 fat
Fiber	3 g		
Sodium	217 mg		

Cranberry Holiday Mold

2 cups boiling water

1 package (8-serving size) or 2 packages (4-serving size each) Jell-O®
   Brand Cranberry Flavor Gelatin Dessert

1½ cups cold sugar-free ginger ale or water

2 cups halved green and/or red seedless grapes

1 can (11 ounces) mandarin orange segments, drained

1. In large bowl, stir boiling water into gelatin for 2 minutes or until completely dissolved.
2. Stir in cold ginger ale. Refrigerate about 1½ hours or until thickened (spoon drawn through leaves a definite impression).
3. Stir in fruit. Spoon into 5-cup mold.
4. Refrigerate 4 hours or until firm.
5. Unmold. Garnish as desired. Store leftover mold in refrigerator.

Serves: 7   Serving size: ¾ cup

Tip

Before unmolding, dip mold in hot water for about 15 seconds. Gently pull gelatin from around edges with moist fingers. Place moistened serving plate on top of mold. Invert mold and plate; holding mold and plate together, shake slightly to loosen. Gently remove mold and center gelatin on plate.

NUTRITION FACTS PER SERVING

Calories	79	Carbohydrate choices	1
Carbohydrate	20 g		
Protein	1 g	Exchanges	1 fruit
Fat	<1 g		
Saturated fat	0 g		
Fiber	<1 g		
Sodium	33 mg		

Meat Entrees

Easy Meat Loaf

2 pounds extra-lean ground beef
1 package (6¼ ounces) Stove Top® Stuffing Mix for Beef
1 cup water
½ cup ketchup, divided
2 eggs, beaten

1. Preheat oven to 375° F. Mix all ingredients except ¼ cup of the ketchup.
2. Shape meat mixture into oval loaf in 12 x 8-inch baking dish; top with remaining ¼ cup ketchup.
3. Bake 1 hour or until center is no longer pink.

Serves: 8   Serving size: ⅛ recipe

NUTRITION FACTS PER SERVING

Calories	269	*Carbohydrate choices*	1½
Carbohydrate	21 g		
Protein	29 g	*Exchanges*	1½ starch
Fat	7 g		3 lean meat
Saturated fat	2 g		
Fiber	1 g		
Sodium	595 mg		

Home-style Beef Brisket

1 envelope Lipton® Recipe Secrets® Onion Soup Mix
³/₄ cup water
½ cup ketchup
1 teaspoon Lawry's® Garlic Powder and Parsley
½ teaspoon ground black pepper
1 brisket (3 pounds) of beef

1. Preheat oven to 325° F. Blend soup mix, water, ketchup, garlic powder and pepper. Place in a 13 x 9-inch baking or roasting pan.
2. Add brisket, turning to coat with soup mixture. Loosely cover with aluminum foil and roast 3 hours or until brisket is tender. Thicken gravy, if desired.

Serves: 10   Serving size: ¹/₁₀ recipe

Variations

Substitute Lipton® Recipe Secrets® Onion-Mushroom or Beefy Onion Soup Mix for Onion Soup Mix.

NUTRITION FACTS PER SERVING

Calories   235

Carbohydrate   5 g

Protein   30 g

Fat   10 g

Saturated fat   4 g

Fiber   1 g

Sodium   561 mg

Carbohydrate choices   0

Exchanges   4 lean meat

No-mess Savory Steak

1 chuck or round steak (2 pounds), about 2 inches thick, trimmed of fat
1 envelope Lipton® Recipe Secrets® Onion Soup Mix

1. Preheat oven to 375° F. Place steak on 18 x 18-inch piece of heavy-duty aluminum foil.
2. Sprinkle both sides of steak with soup mix. Wrap foil loosely around steak, sealing edges airtight with double fold.
3. Place in 13 x 9-inch baking or roasting pan and bake 1 hour or until steak is tender. Thicken gravy, if desired, and pour over steak.

Serves: 10   Serving size: 1/10 recipe

Variations

Substitute Lipton® Recipe Secrets® Italian Herb with Tomato or Onion-Mushroom Soup Mix for Onion Soup Mix.

NUTRITION FACTS PER SERVING

Calories	185	*Carbohydrate choices*	0
Carbohydrate	2 g		
Protein	19 g	*Exchanges*	3 lean meat
Fat	11 g		
Saturated fat	4 g		
Fiber	<1 g		
Sodium	393 mg		

Steak in Mushroom Onion Gravy ◔

4 boneless beef cubed steaks (about 1 pound)
1 tablespoon vegetable oil
1 large onion, halved, thinly sliced
1 jar (12 ounces) Heinz® Fat Free Mushroom Gravy
2 cups cooked noodles

1. In skillet, quickly brown beef in oil about 1 minute per side; remove.
2. Add onion and cook until crisp-tender.
3. Stir in gravy. Return beef to skillet; simmer 2 to 3 minutes.
4. Serve each steak with ½ cup hot noodles and ½ cup gravy.

Serves: 4   Serving size: 1 steak

NUTRITION FACTS PER SERVING

Calories	355	*Carbohydrate choices*	2
Carbohydrate	28 g		
Protein	30 g	*Exchanges*	2 starch
Fat	13 g		3 lean meat
Saturated fat	4 g		
Fiber	2 g		
Sodium	552 mg		

Oriental Beef Lo Mein ℚ

8 ounces uncooked vermicelli or spaghetti
¾ cup Land O Lakes® Light Sour Cream
1 envelope (1 to 1.5 ounces) stir-fry seasoning mix
1 tablespoon sesame oil or vegetable oil
¾ pound pre-cut beef stir-fry meat
1 teaspoon finely chopped fresh garlic
4 cups broccoli coleslaw mix (available in produce section of supermarket)
1 medium red pepper, cut into thin strips

1. Cook pasta according to package directions. Rinse with hot water;
   drain.
2. Meanwhile, in small bowl stir together sour cream and stir-fry seasoning mix until well blended; set aside.
3. Heat oil in Dutch oven; add beef strips and garlic. Cook over medium-
   high heat, stirring constantly, until beef is no longer pink (2 to 3
   minutes).
4. Add broccoli coleslaw mix and red pepper; continue cooking, stirring
   constantly, until vegetables are crisp-tender (1 to 2 minutes).
5. Reduce heat to low; stir in sour cream mixture. Continue cooking until
   heated through (1 minute).
6. Add pasta; toss to coat well.

Serves: 6   Serving size: ⅙ recipe

NUTRITION FACTS PER SERVING

Calories	345	*Carbohydrate choices*	2½
Carbohydrate	39 g		
Protein	22 g	*Exchanges*	2 starch
Fat	12 g		1 vegetable
Saturated fat	4 g		2 meat
Fiber	4 g		
Sodium	314 mg		

Beef Teriyaki ☉

2 cups uncooked Minute® Original Rice
1 pound beef sirloin steak, cut into strips
1 tablespoon vegetable oil
3 cups fresh or frozen stir-fry vegetables, thawed if frozen
¾ cup teriyaki baste and glaze sauce

1. Cook rice according to package directions. Set aside and keep hot.
2. Heat oil in large skillet. Stir-fry meat in hot oil for 5 minutes.
3. Add vegetables and sauce; cover. Simmer 3 to 4 minutes or until vegetables are crisp-tender, stirring frequently. Serve over hot rice.

Serves: 6   Serving size: ⅙ recipe

NUTRITION FACTS PER SERVING

Calories	319	*Carbohydrate choices*	3
Carbohydrate	46 g		
Protein	21 g	*Exchanges*	3 starch
Fat	5 g		1 vegetable
Saturated fat	1 g		2 lean meat
Fiber	2 g		
Sodium	1280 mg		

Asian Beef & Noodles

1¼ pounds extra-lean ground beef
2 packages (2.8 ounces each) baked Oriental flavor ramen noodle soup
2 cups water
2 cups frozen mixed vegetables
¼ teaspoon ground ginger
2 tablespoons thinly sliced green onion

1. In large nonstick skillet, brown ground beef over medium heat 8 to 10 minutes or until no longer pink, breaking up into ¾-inch crumbles. Remove with slotted spoon; pour off fat. Season beef with 1 seasoning packet from noodles; set aside.
2. In same skillet, combine water, noodles (broken into several pieces), vegetables, ginger and remaining seasoning packet. Bring to a boil; reduce heat. Cover; simmer 3 minutes or until noodles are tender, stirring occasionally.
3. Return beef to skillet; heat through. Stir in green onion before serving.

Serves: 6   Serving size: ⅙ recipe

NUTRITION FACTS PER SERVING

Calories	282	*Carbohydrate choices*	1½
Carbohydrate	23 g		
Protein	23 g	*Exchanges*	1½ starch
Fat	11 g		3 lean meat
Saturated fat	4 g		
Fiber	2 g		
Sodium	578 mg		

Vegetable Stir-fry with Noodles and Ground Beef ©

2 tablespoons vegetable oil
1 pound extra-lean ground beef
1 bag (16 ounces) frozen Flav-R-Pac® Vegetable Stir-Fry with Noodles®
¼ cup light soy sauce

1. Heat oil in wok or large skillet over medium-high heat.
2. Add ground beef and stir-fry until browned; drain fat, then push ground beef to side of wok or skillet.
3. Add frozen vegetables and noodles and stir-fry about 4 minutes.
4. Add soy sauce and stir-fry ground beef, vegetables and noodles together for 1 minute or until mixture is coated.

Serves: 4   Serving size: 1

NUTRITION FACTS PER SERVING

Calories	286	*Carbohydrate choices*	1
Carbohydrate	16 g		
Protein	29 g	*Exchanges*	1 starch
Fat	12 g		1 vegetable
Saturated fat	2 g		3 lean meat
Fiber	6 g		
Sodium	689 mg		

Sloppy Joe Pizza

1 pound extra-lean ground beef
³/₄ cup frozen corn, thawed
³/₄ cup barbecue sauce
½ cup sliced green onions
1 (12-inch diameter) Italian bread shell or prepared pizza crust
1½ cups (6 ounces) shredded Co-Jack cheese

1. Preheat oven to 425° F. In large nonstick skillet, brown ground beef over medium heat 8 to 10 minutes or until no longer pink, stirring occasionally; drain.
2. Stir in corn, barbecue sauce and green onions; heat through.
3. Place bread shell on large baking sheet. Top evenly with beef mixture; sprinkle with cheese. Bake 12 to 16 minutes or until cheese is melted; cut into 8 wedges.

Serves: 8   Serving size: 1 wedge

NUTRITION FACTS PER SERVING

Calories	431	*Carbohydrate choices*	2½
Carbohydrate	40 g		
Protein	22 g	*Exchanges*	2½ starch
Fat	20 g		2 meat
Saturated fat	8 g		2 fat
Fiber	2 g		
Sodium	935 mg		

Easy Pasta Bake

1 pound extra-lean ground beef
5 cups cooked pasta
1 jar (27 to 32 ounces) spaghetti sauce
½ cup Kraft® 100% Grated Parmesan Cheese
1 package (8 ounces) Kraft® Shredded Part Skim Mozzarella Cheese

1. Preheat oven to 375° F. Cook ground beef in large skillet; drain.
2. Stir in pasta, spaghetti sauce and parmesan cheese.
3. Spoon into 13 x 9-inch baking dish. Top with mozzarella cheese. Bake 20 minutes or until heated through.

Serves: 8   Serving size: ⅛ recipe

NUTRITION FACTS PER SERVING

Calories	368	*Carbohydrate choices* 2½	
Carbohydrate	36 g		
Protein	27 g	*Exchanges* 2½ starch	
Fat	12 g	3 lean meat	
Saturated fat	5 g		
Fiber	3 g		
Sodium	996 mg		

Taco Cheeseburgers ⊙

1 pound extra-lean ground beef
1 package (1¼ ounces) taco seasoning mix
4 Kraft® Singles Process American Cheese Food
4 kaiser rolls or hamburger buns, split and toasted
Leaf lettuce, picante sauce or salsa, chopped onion, sour cream, guacamole,
*   sliced olives or jalapeño pepper slices for garnish, optional*

1. Mix ground beef and seasoning mix. Shape into 4 patties.
2. Grill or broil patties 4 to 6 minutes on each side, or until done.
3. Top each patty with 1 cheese food slice. Continue cooking until cheese food is melted.
4. Place each cheeseburger in a roll and top with garnishes, if desired.

Serves: 4   Serving size: 1 sandwich

NUTRITION FACTS PER SERVING

Calories	380	*Carbohydrate choices*	2
Carbohydrate	32 g		
Protein	34 g	*Exchanges*	2 starch
Fat	12 g		4 lean meat
Saturated fat	5 g		
Fiber	2 g		
Sodium	884 mg		

Sloppy Joes ◔

1 pound extra-lean ground beef
¾ cup Pace® Picante Sauce
½ cup barbecue sauce
2 green onions, sliced
5 hamburger buns, split and toasted

1. In skillet over medium-high heat, cook ground beef until browned, stirring to separate meat; drain.
2. Add picante sauce, barbecue sauce and green onions. Mix well.
3. Divide mixture between buns and serve.

Serves: 5   Serving size: 1 sandwich

NUTRITION FACTS PER SERVING

Calories	272	*Carbohydrate choices*	2
Carbohydrate	27 g		
Protein	25 g	*Exchanges*	2 starch
Fat	7 g		3 lean meat
Saturated fat	2 g		
Fiber	2 g		
Sodium	586 mg		

"Messy Hanks" ☯

1 envelope Lipton® Recipe Secrets® Onion Soup Mix
¾ cup chili sauce
¼ cup grape jelly
2 tablespoons water
1 pound extra-lean ground beef
1 medium green pepper, finely chopped
6 hoagie rolls, hamburger buns or English muffins

1. In small bowl, combine soup mix, chili sauce, grape jelly and water.
2. In 10-inch skillet, brown ground beef with green pepper over medium-high heat; drain.
3. Stir in soup mixture. Bring to a boil over high heat. Reduce heat to low and simmer, stirring occasionally, 5 minutes or until slightly thickened.
4. Divide mixture between rolls and serve.

Serves: 6   Serving size: 1 sandwich

Variations

Substitute Lipton® Recipe Secrets® Beefy Onion, Onion-Mushroom or Savory Herb with Garlic Soup Mix for Onion Soup Mix.

NUTRITION FACTS PER SERVING

Calories	442	Carbohydrate choices	4½
Carbohydrate	69 g		
Protein	27 g	Exchanges	4½ starch
Fat	7 g		2 lean meat
Saturated fat	2 g		
Fiber	4 g		
Sodium	1549 mg		

Lipton® Onion Burgers ☺

1 envelope Lipton® Recipe Secrets® Onion Soup Mix
2 pounds extra-lean ground beef
½ cup water

1. In large bowl, combine all ingredients; shape into 8 patties.
2. Grill or broil 4 to 6 minutes on each side, or until done.

Serves: 8   Serving size: 1 burger

Variations

Substitute Lipton® Recipe Secrets® Beefy Onion, Onion-Mushroom or Italian Herb with Tomato Soup Mix for Onion Soup Mix.

NUTRITION FACTS PER SERVING

Calories	165	*Carbohydrate choices*	0
Carbohydrate	3 g		
Protein	26 g	*Exchanges*	4 lean meat
Fat	5 g		
Saturated fat	2 g		
Fiber	1 g		
Sodium	487 mg		

Grilled Reuben Burgers ◔

1 envelope Lipton® Recipe Secrets® Onion-Mushroom Soup Mix
1½ pounds extra-lean ground beef
½ cup water
½ cup (2 ounces) shredded Swiss cheese
1 tablespoon crisp-cooked crumbled bacon or bacon bits
½ teaspoon caraway seeds, optional
6 hamburger buns, split
Sauerkraut, warmed, optional

1. In large bowl, combine soup mix, ground beef, water, cheese, bacon and caraway seeds, if desired. Shape into 6 patties.
2. Grill or broil patties 4 to 6 minutes on each side, or until done.
3. Place each patty in a bun and top with warmed sauerkraut, if desired.

Serves: 6   Serving size: 1 burger

NUTRITION FACTS PER SERVING

Calories	332	*Carbohydrate choices*	1½
Carbohydrate	25 g		
Protein	33 g	*Exchanges*	1½ starch
Fat	10 g		4 lean meat
Saturated fat	4 g		
Fiber	2 g		
Sodium	910 mg		

Pork Tenderloin with Raisin Sauce ☺

1 pound pork tenderloin, trimmed of fat
Vegetable cooking spray
1 jar (12 ounces) Heinz® Fat Free Beef Gravy
⅓ cup golden raisins
3 tablespoons apple jelly
Dash of pepper
1 tablespoon Dijon-style mustard

1. Cut pork into 8 pieces; pound each piece to ½-inch thickness. Spray skillet with cooking spray. Quickly brown pork in skillet, about 1 minute per side.
2. Stir in gravy, raisins, jelly and pepper. Simmer 10 minutes or until pork is no longer pink, stirring sauce and turning pork occasionally.
3. Remove pork. Add mustard to sauce, stirring until blended. Serve sauce over pork.

Serves: 4   Serving size: ¼ recipe

NUTRITION FACTS PER SERVING

Calories	252	Carbohydrate choices	1½
Carbohydrate	24 g		
Protein	27 g	Exchanges	½ starch
Fat	5 g		1 fruit
Saturated fat	2 g		3 lean meat
Fiber	1 g		
Sodium	594 mg		

Southern Skillet BBQ Pork

¼ cup light Italian dressing
¼ cup barbecue sauce
1 teaspoon chili powder
4 boneless pork loin chops (4 ounces each), ¾-inch thick, trimmed of fat

1. Blend dressing, barbecue sauce and chili powder in shallow dish. Add pork chops; turn to coat. Cover; marinate 30 minutes to overnight in refrigerator.
2. Heat nonstick skillet over medium-high heat until hot. Drain pork, reserving marinade. Brown both sides of pork in skillet; add reserved marinade.
3. Bring to a boil. Cover and reduce heat to low; simmer for 5 minutes.

Serves: 4   Serving size: 1 chop

NUTRITION FACTS PER SERVING

Calories 224   *Carbohydrate choices* 0
Carbohydrate 3 g
Protein 24 g   *Exchanges* 3 meat
Fat 12 g
Saturated fat 3 g
Fiber <1 g
Sodium 278 mg

Glazed Pork Chops

²⁄₃ *cup apricot or peach preserves*
¹⁄₂ *cup Wish-Bone® Robusto Fat Free Italian Dressing*
2 *tablespoons Dijon-style mustard*
4 *pork chops, about 1-inch thick (about 1¹⁄₂ pounds), trimmed of fat*

1. For marinade, blend preserves, dressing and mustard.
2. In large, shallow non-aluminum baking dish or plastic bag, pour ³⁄₄ cup of the marinade over chops; turn to coat. Cover, or close bag, and marinate in refrigerator, turning occasionally, 3 hours to overnight. Refrigerate remaining marinade (about ¹⁄₂ cup).
3. Remove chops from marinade, discarding marinade. Grill or broil chops, turning once and brushing frequently with refrigerated marinade, until chops are done.

Serves: 4   Serving size: 1 pork chop

Variation

For baked glazed pork chops, prepare ¹⁄₂ the amount of the marinade as above. Marinate chops as above. Place chops in baking dish with marinade and bake at 425° F, basting occasionally, for 35 minutes or until done.

NUTRITION FACTS PER SERVING

Calories	233	*Carbohydrate choices*	¹⁄₂
Carbohydrate	9 g		
Protein	27 g	*Exchanges*	¹⁄₂ fruit
Fat	9 g		4 lean meat
Saturated fat	3 g		
Fiber	<1 g		
Sodium	148 mg		

Pork Chops with Dijon & Applesauce

1 teaspoon garlic powder
Salt and pepper to taste
1 tablespoon vegetable oil
6 medium-thick pork chops, trimmed of fat
1 cup unsweetened Seneca® Applesauce
1 tablespoon Dijon mustard

1. Sprinkle garlic powder, salt and pepper evenly over both sides of pork chops.
2. Heat oil in large skillet. Brown chops on both sides over high heat.
3. Mix together the applesauce and mustard. Reduce heat to low; pour applesauce mixture over chops. Simmer 20 minutes, or until done.

Serves: 6   Serving size: 1 pork chop

Serving Suggestion

May be served with noodles or rice, and topped with extra sauce.

NUTRITION FACTS PER SERVING

Calories	209	*Carbohydrate choices*	0
Carbohydrate	5 g		
Protein	23 g	*Exchanges*	3 lean meat
Fat	1C g		
Saturated fat	3 g		
Fiber	1 g		
Sodium	73 mg		

Sweet and Sour Pork ◔

1 to 2 tablespoons cornstarch
2 tablespoons water
1 tablespoon vinegar
1 tablespoon soy sauce
¼ cup brown sugar
½ pound pork tenderloin
1 teaspoon oil
1 package frozen Freshlike® Pepper Stir Fry
1 tablespoon water
1 can (8 ounces) pineapple chunks, packed in juice, undrained
2 cups cooked rice

1. In small bowl, combine cornstarch, 2 tablespoons water, vinegar, soy sauce and brown sugar. Stir well. Set aside.
2. Cut pork into thin strips. In large skillet, stir-fry pork in hot oil until cooked.
3. Add frozen stir-fry and 1 tablespoon water. Cover and cook 5 to 7 minutes over medium heat.
4. Uncover and stir in cornstarch mixture, and cook until thickened.
5. Add pineapple chunks with juice. Heat through. Serve at once over hot rice.

Serves: 4   Serving size: ¼ recipe

NUTRITION FACTS PER SERVING

Calories	303	*Carbohydrate choices* 3½	
Carbohydrate	52 g		
Protein	16 g	*Exchanges*	3 starch
Fat	4 g		1 vegetable
Saturated fat	1 g		1 lean meat
Fiber	2 g		
Sodium	592 mg		

Chicken and Turkey Entrees

Parmesan Chicken Pilaf

1 cup Uncle Ben's® Specialty Rices Pilaf
2 cups chicken broth
1 tablespoon margarine or butter
1 tablespoon chopped garlic
1 pound boneless, skinless chicken breast, cut into strips
2 cups fresh or frozen chopped broccoli, thawed and drained if frozen
¼ cup grated Parmesan cheese

1. Cook pilaf according to package directions, using the 2 cups chicken broth and no added fat or salt.
2. In large skillet, heat margarine; add garlic and chicken, and sauté until tender. Add broccoli and sauté until crisp-tender.
3. Stir chicken mixture into cooked pilaf and sprinkle with grated cheese.

Serves: 4   Serving size: 1

NUTRITION FACTS PER SERVING

Calories	431	*Carbohydrate choices* 3	
Carbohydrate	50 g		
Protein	35 g	*Exchanges*	3 starch
Fat	9 g		1 vegetable
Saturated fat	3 g		3 lean meat
Fiber	2 g		
Sodium	708 mg		

Grilled Greek-style Chicken

1 container (8 ounces) plain nonfat yogurt
¼ cup chopped fresh mint or parsley leaves
1 envelope Lipton® Recipe Secrets® Savory Herb with Garlic Soup Mix
1 pound boneless, skinless chicken-breast halves

1. In small, shallow glass baking dish, blend yogurt, mint and soup mix. Add chicken and turn to coat.
2. Cover and marinate in refrigerator, turning chicken occasionally, at least 2 hours.
3. Remove chicken, reserving marinade. Grill or broil chicken, turning once and basting with reserved marinade, until chicken is done.

Serves: 4   Serving size: ¼ recipe

NUTRITION FACTS PER SERVING

Calories	193	*Carbohydrate choices*	½
Carbohydrate	10 g		
Protein	29 g	*Exchanges*	½ starch
Fat	4 g		4 very lean meat
Saturated fat	1 g		
Fiber	1 g		
Sodium	973 mg		

Quick Chicken Marinara

1 tablespoon olive oil
2 boneless, skinless chicken-breast halves (about ¾ pound), cut into strips
1 yellow or green pepper, cut into strips
1 package (15 ounces) Di Giorno® Marinara Sauce
1 package (9 ounces) Di Giorno® Spinach Fettuccine, cooked
Di Giorno® Shredded Parmesan Cheese, optional

1. Heat oil in skillet on medium-high heat. Add chicken and pepper; cook and stir 3 minutes.
2. Stir in sauce. Cook on medium heat 3 to 5 minutes or until chicken is cooked through.
3. Serve over hot fettuccine. Top with shredded cheese, if desired.

Serves: 4   Serving size: ¼ recipe

NUTRITION FACTS PER SERVING

Calories	387	*Carbohydrate choices*	3
Carbohydrate	50 g		
Protein	28 g	*Exchanges*	3 starch
Fat	8 g		3 lean meat
Saturated fat	2 g		
Fiber	4 g		
Sodium	5 9 mg		

Spicy Cranberry Chicken ©

½ cup Heinz® Chili Sauce
½ cup whole berry cranberry sauce
2 tablespoons orange marmalade
⅛ teaspoon ground allspice
6 boneless, skinless chicken-breast halves
2 teaspoons vegetable oil

1. Combine first 4 ingredients; set aside.
2. In large skillet, slowly brown chicken on both sides in oil. Pour chili sauce mixture over chicken.
3. Simmer, uncovered, 8 to 10 minutes or until chicken is cooked and sauce is desired consistency. Turn and baste occasionally.

Serves: 6   Serving size: 1 chicken breast

NUTRITION FACTS PER SERVING

Calories	219	*Carbohydrate choices*	1
Carbohydrate	19 g		
Protein	25 g	*Exchanges*	1 fruit
Fat	5 g		4 very lean meat
Saturated fat	1 g		
Fiber	1 g		
Sodium	303 mg		

Chicken Picante

½ cup chunky picante sauce
¼ cup Dijon-style mustard
2 tablespoons lime juice
6 boneless, skinless chicken-breast halves
2 tablespoons margarine or butter
Chopped cilantro for garnish
Plain nonfat yogurt, optional

1. Combine picante sauce, mustard and lime juice in large bowl. Add chicken, turning to coat. Cover; marinate in refrigerator at least 30 minutes.
2. Melt margarine in large skillet over medium heat until foamy.
3. Remove chicken from marinade; reserve marinade. Add chicken to skillet; cook about 10 minutes or until brown on both sides.
4. Add marinade; cook about 5 minutes or until chicken is tender and marinade glazes chicken.
5. Remove chicken to serving platter. Boil marinade over high heat 1 minute; pour over chicken.
6. Garnish with cilantro. Serve each piece of chicken with 1 tablespoon yogurt, if desired.

Serves: 6   Serving size: 1 chicken-breast half

NUTRITION FACTS PER SERVING

Calories	190	*Carbohydrate choices*	0
Carbohydrate	2 g		
Protein	27 g	*Exchanges*	4 lean meat
Fat	8 g		
Saturated fat	2 g		
Fiber	1 g		
Sodium	304 mg		

Southwestern Chicken Rolls

1 package (10 tortillas) Buena Vida™ Fat Free Flour Tortillas
Vegetable cooking spray
½ cup chopped onion
1 garlic clove, minced
2 cups (16 ounces) prepared salsa, divided
½ teaspoon chili powder
2 cups finely chopped, cooked chicken breast
1½ cups small curd low-fat cottage cheese
1½ cups shredded mozzarella cheese, divided

1. Remove tortillas from refrigerator; set aside. Preheat oven to 350° F.
2. Heat large nonstick skillet that has been lightly coated with cooking spray. Cook onion and garlic for 2 to 3 minutes or until tender.
3. Stir in ½ cup salsa, chili powder and chicken. Heat for 5 minutes, stirring occasionally. Remove from heat.
4. Stir in cottage cheese and ½ cup mozzarella cheese.
5. Heat tortillas according to package directions. Place approximately ⅓ cup filling in center of tortilla. Roll up tortilla and place seam side down in a 9 x 13-inch baking dish that has been lightly sprayed with cooking spray. Repeat with remaining tortillas and filling.
6. Pour remaining 1½ cups salsa over rolled tortillas. Top with remaining 1 cup mozzarella cheese. Bake 15 to 20 minutes or until cheese is bubbly and filling is hot.

Serves: 10   Serving size: 1 roll

NUTRITION FACTS PER SERVING

Calories	214	*Carbohydrate choices*	1
Carbohydrate	18 g		
Protein	20 g	*Exchanges*	1 starch
Fat	6 g		2 lean meat
Saturated fat	3 g		
Fiber	2 g		
Sodium	494 mg		

Wild Roasted Chicken Wraps

1 box (16 ounces) Uncle Ben's® Long Grain & Wild Rice
2 cups diced cooked chicken breast
½ cup light ranch salad dressing
12 flour tortillas
1 cup shredded lettuce

1. Cook rice according to package directions, without any added butter or margarine.
2. Mix chicken and ranch dressing with cooked rice.
3. Spoon ⅓ cup rice mixture onto each flat tortilla. Top with lettuce. Roll tortilla and secure with toothpicks.

Serves: 12   Serving size: 1 tortilla

NUTRITION FACTS PER SERVING

Calories	186	*Carbohydrate choices*	1½
Carbohydrate	24 g		
Protein	11 g	*Exchanges*	1½ starch
Fat	5 g		1 meat
Saturated fat	1 g		
Fiber	1 g		
Sodium	362 mg		

Easy Chicken & Noodles ①

1 pound boneless, skinless chicken breast, cut into bite-sized pieces
1 can (10¾ ounces) Campbell's® Condensed 98% Fat Free Cream of
    Mushroom Soup
1¾ cups water
2 cups frozen vegetable mix (broccoli, cauliflower and carrots)
2 packages (2.8 ounces each) Campbell's® Baked Chicken Flavor Ramen
    Noodle Soup

1. In nonstick skillet over medium-high heat, cook chicken until
   browned, stirring often. Set aside.
2. Add mushroom soup, water, vegetables and 1 Ramen seasoning packet
   to skillet. (Reserve remaining seasoning packet for another use.) Heat
   to a boil. Cook over medium heat 5 minutes, stirring often.
3. Break up noodles from both noodle packages and add to skillet. Return
   chicken to skillet. Cook 5 minutes or until noodles are done, stirring
   thoroughly to separate noodles.

Serves: 4   Serving size: ¼ recipe

NUTRITION FACTS PER SERVING

Calories	335	*Carbohydrate choices*	2½
Carbohydrate	40 g		
Protein	30 g	*Exchanges*	2 starch
Fat	6 g		1 vegetable
Saturated fat	2 g		3 lean meat
Fiber	3 g		
Sodium	1124 mg		

Chicken Broccoli Divan

1 pound fresh broccoli, cut into spears, cooked and drained or 1 package (10 ounces) frozen broccoli spears, cooked and drained

1½ cups cubed cooked chicken or turkey

1 can (10¾ ounces) Campbell's® Condensed 98% Fat Free Broccoli Cheese Soup

⅓ cup skim milk

2 tablespoons crushed corn flakes

1. Preheat oven to 400° F. In 9-inch pie plate or 2-quart shallow baking dish arrange broccoli and chicken.
2. Mix soup and milk and pour over broccoli and chicken.
3. Sprinkle corn flake crumbs over top. Bake 25 minutes or until hot.

Serves: 4   Serving size: ¼ recipe

NUTRITION FACTS PER SERVING

Calories	162	*Carbohydrate choices*	1
Carbohydrate	13 g		
Protein	20 g	*Exchanges*	½ starch
Fat	4 g		1 vegetable
Saturated fat	1 g		2 lean meat
Fiber	3 g		
Sodium	361 mg		

Fabulous 15-Minute Chicken à la King ☺

1 cup Land O Lakes® Light Sour Cream

2 tablespoons all-purpose flour

3 cups frozen vegetable mix (broccoli, carrots, water chestnuts and red pepper)

¼ pound deli cooked chicken or turkey breast, cubed

1 can (10½ ounces) condensed chicken broth

Salt and pepper to taste

3 English muffins, split and toasted

1. In small bowl, with wire whisk, stir together sour cream and flour until smooth; set aside.
2. In 4-quart saucepan combine frozen vegetables, chicken and chicken broth. Cook over medium-high heat, stirring occasionally, until vegetables are crisp-tender (4 to 5 minutes). Reduce heat to medium.
3. Add sour cream mixture. Continue cooking, stirring constantly, until mixture thickens and just comes to a boil (1 to 2 minutes). Remove from heat; stir in salt and pepper to taste.
4. Serve hot mixture over toasted English muffins.

Serves: 6   Serving size: ⅙ recipe

NUTRITION FACTS PER SERVING

Calories	188	*Carbohydrate choices*	1½
Carbohydrate	25 g		
Protein	14 g	*Exchanges*	1 starch
Fat	4 g		1 vegetable
Saturated fat	2 g		1 lean meat
Fiber	3 g		
Sodium	416 mg		

Asian Chicken & Noodles

1 package (3 ounces) chicken flavor instant ramen noodles
2 cups water
1 bag (16 ounces) frozen Birds Eye® Farm Fresh Mixtures Broccoli, Carrots and Water Chestnuts
1 tablespoon vegetable oil
1 pound boneless, skinless chicken breast, cut into thin strips
¼ cup stir-fry sauce

1. Reserve seasoning packet from ramen noodles. Bring water to a boil in large saucepan. Add noodles and frozen vegetables. Cook 3 minutes, stirring occasionally; drain.
2. Meanwhile, heat oil in large nonstick skillet over medium-high heat. Add chicken; cook and stir until browned, about 8 minutes.
3. Stir in noodles and vegetables, stir-fry sauce and reserved seasoning packet; heat through.

Serves: 4   Serving size: ¼ recipe

NUTRITION FACTS PER SERVING

Calories	301	*Carbohydrate choices*	1½
Carbohydrate	23 g		
Protein	29 g	*Exchanges*	1 starch
Fat	10 g		1 vegetable
Saturated fat	2 g		3 lean meat
Fiber	4 g		
Sodium	1105 mg		

Catalina Chicken Stir-fry ⊙

¾ *cup Kraft® Light or Fat Free Catalina French Dressing*
¼ *cup light soy sauce*
½ *teaspoon garlic powder*
1 pound boneless, skinless chicken breast, cubed
1 package (16 ounces) frozen mixed vegetables, any variety, thawed,
  or 3 cups fresh-cut vegetables
3 cups cooked Minute® Rice

1. Heat dressing, soy sauce and garlic powder in large skillet.
2. Stir in chicken. Cook until chicken is done, about 8 minutes.
3. Add vegetables; stir until cooked through.
4. Serve over hot rice.

Serves: 6   Serving size: 1

NUTRITION FACTS PER SERVING

Calories	275	*Carbohydrate choices*	2
Carbohydrate	34 g		
Protein	21 g	*Exchanges*	2 starch
Fat	6 g		1 vegetable
Saturated fat	1 g		2 lean meat
Fiber	2 g		
Sodium	1171 mg		

Shake 'N Bake® Chicken Nuggets ☺

5 boneless, skinless chicken-breast halves, cut into 1½- to 2-inch pieces
1 packet Shake 'N Bake® Seasoning and Coating Mixture, Original Recipe
    for Chicken
Vegetable cooking spray
Kraft® Original Barbecue Sauce, optional
Honey, optional

1. Preheat oven to 400° F. Shake chicken pieces with coating mixture;
   discard any remaining mixture.
2. Place on shallow baking pan that has been sprayed with cooking spray.
   Bake 10 to 15 minutes or until cooked through.
3. Serve with barbecue sauce and honey, if desired.

Serves: 6   Serving size: ⅙ recipe

NUTRITION FACTS PER SERVING

Calories	164		
Carbohydrate	9 g	*Carbohydrate choices*	½
Protein	22 g		
Fat	4 g	*Exchanges*	½ starch
Saturated fat	1 g		3 very lean meat
Fiber	0 g		
Sodium	353 mg		

Turkey Potato Loaf
with Red Pepper Cream

1½ *pounds ground turkey*
1½ *cups refrigerated shredded potatoes*
1 *medium onion, chopped*
¼ *cup chopped fresh basil leaves or 1 tablespoon dried basil*
½ *teaspoon salt*
¼ *teaspoon pepper*
¾ *cup Land O Lakes® Light Sour Cream*
⅓ *cup skim milk*
⅓ *cup roasted red peppers, drained and finely chopped*
¼ *teaspoon garlic powder*

1. Preheat oven to 350° F. In large bowl, stir together turkey, potatoes, onion, basil, salt and pepper. Press into 8 x 4-inch loaf pan. Bake for 45 to 50 minutes or until well browned.
2. In 1-quart saucepan stir together sour cream and milk with wire whisk until smooth. Stir in red peppers and garlic powder. Cook over medium heat, stirring constantly, until heated through. Serve sliced turkey loaf with red pepper cream sauce.

Serves: 8   Serving size: ⅛ recipe

NUTRITION FACTS PER SERVING

Calories	237	*Carbohydrate choices*	1
Carbohydrate	15 g		
Protein	20 g	*Exchanges*	1 starch
Fat	11 g		2 meat
Saturated fat	4 g		
Fiber	1 g		
Sodium	228 mg		

Sweet Potato Turkey Pie

1 can (24 ounces) sweet potatoes, drained
2 tablespoons margarine, melted
¼ teaspoon pumpkin pie spice
Vegetable cooking spray
2 cups cooked turkey, cut into ½- to ¾-inch cubes
1 can (10¾ ounces) 98% fat-free cream of mushroom soup
1 package (9 ounces) frozen French-style green beans, thawed and drained
1 can (2 ounces) mushroom stems and pieces, drained
½ teaspoon salt
½ teaspoon pepper
2 tablespoons canned fried onion rings, crushed
1 can (8 ounces) cranberry sauce, optional

1. Preheat oven to 350° F. In medium bowl, blend sweet potatoes, margarine and pumpkin pie spice until smooth. Coat a 9-inch pie plate lightly with cooking spray, and line plate with potato mixture to form a "pie shell"; set aside.
2. In medium bowl, combine turkey, soup, beans, mushrooms, salt and pepper. Pour mixture into prepared shell.
3. Sprinkle onions over top. Bake 30 minutes or until hot. Serve with cranberry sauce, if desired.

Serves: 6   Serving size: ⅙ recipe

NUTRITION FACTS PER SERVING

Calories 250
Carbohydrate 31 g
Protein 15 g
Fat 8 g
Saturated fat 2 g
Fiber 5 g
Sodium 764 mg

Carbohydrate choices 2

Exchanges 2 starch
1 vegetable
1 meat

Turkey Pizza Foldovers

4 Azteca® Flour Tortillas
1/2 cup pizza sauce
1/2 pound lean ground turkey, browned and drained
1 cup shredded part-skim mozzarella cheese
Vegetable cooking spray

1. Preheat oven to 375° F. Heat tortillas according to package directions. Keep covered until ready to use.
2. Mix together pizza sauce and browned ground turkey. Spread half of each tortilla with the sauce and turkey mixture.
3. Top each tortilla with 1/4 cup shredded cheese.
4. Fold tortilla in half. Place on baking sheet sprayed with cooking spray. Bake for 9 to 11 minutes or until edges are golden brown.

Serves: 4 *Serving size: 1 foldover*

NUTRITION FACTS PER SERVING

Calories	266	*Carbohydrate choices*	1
Carbohydrate	16 g		
Protein	22 g	*Exchanges*	1 starch
Fat	12 g		3 lean meat
Saturated fat	5 g		
Fiber	1 g		
Sodium	434 mg		

BBQ Turkey Buns ◔

*6 ounces Jennie-O® Mesquite Bar-B-Q Flavored Marinated Turkey Breast,
   cut into ½-inch strips*
½ cup barbecue sauce
2 tablespoons chopped onion
4 hamburger buns, split
½ cup shredded mozzarella cheese

1. In small saucepan over medium heat, stir together turkey strips, barbecue sauce and onion. Cook and stir about 5 minutes or until mixture is
   hot.
2. Divide mixture evenly among 4 bun halves. Top each with 2 tablespoons
   cheese. Replace bun tops.

Serves: 4   Serving size: 1 sandwich

NUTRITION FACTS PER SERVING

Calories	234	*Carbohydrate choices*	2
Carbohydrate	27 g		
Protein	15 g	*Exchanges*	2 starch
Fat	6 g		1 meat
Saturated fat	3 g		
Fiber	2 g		
Sodium	1091 mg		

Smoked Turkey Tostadas ◐

½ pound deli smoked turkey breast, cut into ½-inch cubes
½ cup chunky salsa
1 can (15 ounces) black beans, rinsed and drained
1 can (11 ounces) whole kernel corn with green and red peppers
¾ cup Land O Lakes® Light Sour Cream
12 tostada shells or taco shells
Sliced green onions, chopped tomatoes, and shredded lettuce for toppings,
    optional

1. In small bowl, stir together turkey, salsa, black beans and corn; set
   aside.
2. To assemble tostadas, spread each tostada shell with 1 tablespoon sour
   cream; top with about ⅓ cup turkey mixture. Sprinkle with desired
   toppings.

Serves: 6   Serving size: 2 tostadas

NUTRITION FACTS PER SERVING

Calories	346	*Carbohydrate choices*	3
Carbohydrate	50 g		
Protein	18 g	*Exchanges*	3 starch
Fat	10 g		1 meat
Saturated fat	3 g		
Fiber	9 g		
Sodium	935 mg		

Easy Barbecued Turkey Joes ☺

1 pound lean ground turkey
½ cup fresh or frozen chopped green pepper
½ cup fresh or frozen chopped red pepper
½ cup fresh or frozen chopped onion
1 cup Kraft® Barbecue Sauce
6 hamburger buns, split
6 slices (¾ ounce each) Kraft® American Singles Pasteurized Process
Cheese Food

1. Brown turkey; drain. Add peppers and onion; cook until tender.
2. Add barbecue sauce; heat thoroughly, stirring occasionally.
3. Top bottom halves of buns with 1 cheese food slice and meat mixture. Cover with top halves of buns.

Serves: 6   Serving size: 1 sandwich

NUTRITION FACTS PER SERVING

Calories	366	*Carbohydrate choices*	2
Carbohydrate	30 g		
Protein	24 g	*Exchanges*	2 starch
Fat	16 g		3 meat
Saturated fat	6 g		
Fiber	2 g		
Sodium	920 mg		

Fish and Seafood Entrees

Pesto Swordfish Steaks ⏱

¼ *cup tightly packed fresh basil leaves*
3 tablespoons fat-free Italian dressing
1 garlic clove, minced
⅛ *teaspoon black pepper*
1 package (12 ounces) Healthy Choice® Swordfish Steaks, thawed

Oven Directions

1. Combine basil, Italian dressing, garlic and pepper in a blender or food processor. Blend until basil is finely chopped.
2. Arrange steaks in baking dish and spread basil mixture on top of steaks.
3. Place 6 inches under broiler for 4 to 5 minutes or until fish is firm and opaque and flakes easily with a fork.

Microwave Directions

1. Combine basil, Italian dressing, garlic and pepper in a blender or food processor. Blend until basil is finely chopped.
2. Arrange steaks in microwave-safe dish and spread basil mixture on top of steaks.
3. Microwave on high for 2½ minutes or until fish is firm and opaque and flakes easily with a fork.

Serves: 2   Serving size: 1 steak

NUTRITION FACTS PER SERVING

Calories	184	*Carbohydrate choices*	0
Carbohydrate	3 g		
Protein	26 g	*Exchanges*	4 lean meat
Fat	7 g		
Saturated fat	2 g		
Fiber	<1 g		
Sodium	276 mg		

Baked Fish Fillets with Peppers

6 fish fillets (4 ounces each) such as catfish, halibut or walleye
Vegetable cooking spray
2 tablespoons reduced-calorie margarine, melted
1 tablespoon lemon juice
¼ teaspoon ground ginger
¼ teaspoon curry powder
1 bag (16 ounces) frozen tri-colored pepper stir-fry mix, thawed

1. Preheat oven to 400° F. Place fish fillets on rack of broiler pan coated with cooking spray.
2. Combine margarine, lemon juice, ginger and curry powder; stir well. Brush fillets with margarine mixture.
3. Top fillets evenly with pepper mixture.
4. Bake 20 to 25 minutes or until fish flakes easily with a fork.

Serves: 6   Serving size: 1 fish fillet

NUTRITION FACTS PER SERVING

Calories	137	*Carbohydrate choices*	0
Carbohydrate	5 g		
Protein	22 g	*Exchanges*	1 vegetable
Fat	3 g		3 very lean meat
Saturated fat	<1 g		
Fiber	2 g		
Sodium	112 mg		

Seafood Marinara ☺

1 package (7 ounces) spaghetti or angel hair pasta
1 jar (2 cups) marinara sauce
1 package (8 ounces) Louis Kemp® Fat Free Scallop, Crab or Lobster
*   Delights®, cut into bite-sized pieces*
Grated Parmesan cheese, optional

1. Prepare pasta according to package directions; drain.
2. In separate pan, heat marinara sauce until warm. Add seafood and cooked pasta to sauce and stir until blended. Top with grated cheese, if desired.

Serves: 6   Serving size: ⅙ recipe

NUTRITION FACTS PER SERVING

Calories	233	*Carbohydrate choices*	2½
Carbohydrate	39 g		
Protein	11 g	*Exchanges*	2½ starch
Fat	4 g		1 very lean meat
Saturated fat	1 g		
Fiber	2 g		
Sodium	847 mg		

Three-cheese Fish and Rice Bake

1 can (1 pound, 1 ounce) Contadina® Dalla Casa Buitoni Country Italian
  Cooking Sauce with Three Cheeses & Herbs
1 can (14½ ounces) chicken broth
1 cup uncooked long-grain white rice
1½ pounds firm white fish fillets, cut into 6 serving-size pieces
6 lemon slices
¼ cup chopped fresh parsley

Oven Directions

1. Preheat oven to 400° F. Combine cooking sauce, broth and rice in
   13 x 9-inch baking dish.
2. Place fish in sauce mixture. Bake, covered, 45 to 50 minutes or until
   rice is tender.
3. Top each serving with lemon slices and sprinkle with parsley.

Microwave Directions

1. Combine cooking sauce, broth and rice in 2½-quart round microwave-
   safe baking dish. Microwave on high (100%) power for 5 minutes.
2. Place fish in sauce mixture. Microwave, covered, on high power for 20
   to 25 minutes or until rice is tender. Cool in baking dish for 5 minutes.
3. Top each serving with lemon slices and sprinkle with parsley.

Serves: 6   Serving size: 1

NUTRITION FACTS PER SERVING

Calories	299	*Carbohydrate choices*	2
Carbohydrate	35 g		
Protein	27 g	*Exchanges*	2 starch
Fat	5 g		1 vegetable
Saturated fat	1 g		3 very lean meat
Fiber	2 g		
Sodium	958 mg		

Shrimp Creole Macaroni ☺

1 package (14 ounces) Kraft® Macaroni & Cheese Dinner
½ cup skim milk
½ cup frozen chopped green pepper
¼ cup frozen chopped onion
1 tablespoon soft reduced-calorie margarine
1 can (14½ ounces) stewed tomatoes, drained and cut up
½ pound cooked shrimp
½ teaspoon hot pepper sauce

1. Prepare macaroni and cheese as directed on package, omitting margarine and using ½ cup skim milk instead.
2. In medium skillet, cook and stir green pepper and onion in margarine until crisp-tender.
3. Add prepared dinner and remaining ingredients; stir on medium heat until thoroughly heated.

Serves: 6   Serving size: 1 cup

NUTRITION FACTS PER SERVING

Calories	209	*Carbohydrate choices* 2
Protein	14 g	
Carbohydrate	28 g	*Exchanges* 2 starch
Fat	4 g	1 lean meat
Saturated fat	1 g	
Fiber	2 g	
Sodium	457 mg	

Creole Red Snapper

Vegetable cooking spray
¼ cup frozen chopped onion
¼ cup frozen chopped green pepper
1 teaspoon minced garlic
1 can (14½ ounces) diced tomatoes, undrained
2 teaspoons Worcestershire sauce
2 teaspoons red wine vinegar
½ teaspoon basil
¼ teaspoon pepper
4 red snapper fillets (4 ounces each)

1. Spray large skillet with cooking spray and heat over medium-high heat until hot. Add onion, green pepper and garlic; sauté until tender, stirring frequently.
2. Add tomatoes with juice and remaining ingredients except fish. Bring to a boil; add fillets, spooning tomato mixture over fish.
3. Reduce heat and simmer, covered, 10 to 12 minutes or until fish flakes easily with a fork.

Serves: 4   Serving size: ¼ recipe

NUTRITION FACTS PER SERVING

Calories	133	*Carbohydrate choices* ½	
Carbohydrate	7 g		
Protein	23 g	*Exchanges*	½ starch or 1 vegetable
Fat	2 g		3 very lean meat
Saturated fat	< 1 g		
Fiber	1 g		
Sodium	285 mg		

Cajun Shrimp Stir-fry ☺

$1/2$ cup water
1 can (6 ounces) tomato paste
2 tablespoons Worcestershire sauce
$1/2$ teaspoon hot pepper sauce
1 medium onion, chopped
4 ribs celery, chopped
1 tablespoon vegetable oil
1 package (16 ounces) frozen Freshlike® Chili Bean Stir Fry
2 tablespoons water
$1/2$ pound cooked shrimp
2 cups cooked rice
$1/4$ cup chopped fresh cilantro, optional

1. In small bowl, combine $1/2$ cup water, tomato paste, Worcestershire sauce and hot pepper sauce. Stir well. Set aside.
2. In large skillet, stir-fry onion and celery in oil until crisp-tender. Add frozen chili bean stir fry and 2 tablespoons water. Cover and cook 7 to 10 minutes.
3. Uncover and stir in reserved sauce mixture. Add cooked shrimp and heat through.
4. Serve over hot rice. Garnish with cilantro, if desired.

Serves: 4   Serving size: $1/4$ recipe

Variation

$1/2$ pound cooked pork, cut into thin strips, may be substituted for shrimp.

NUTRITION FACTS PER SERVING

Calories	311	*Carbohydrate choices*	3
Carbohydrate	50 g		
Protein	19 g	*Exchanges*	3 starch
Fat	5 g		1 vegetable
Saturated fat	1 g		1 lean meat
Fiber	9 g		
Sodium	912 mg		

Albacore Stir-fry ☉

2 tablespoons vegetable oil

½ cup chopped onion

1 large clove garlic, minced

1 bag (16 ounces) frozen Oriental vegetables or 4 cups thinly sliced
   assorted vegetables

1 (12¼ ounces) or 2 (6⅛ ounces) cans Starkist® Solid White Albacore in
   spring water, drained

3 tablespoons light soy sauce

1 teaspoon sugar

1 tablespoon lemon juice

1 tablespoon water

2 cups cooked rice

1. Heat oil in large skillet or wok and stir-fry onion, garlic and vegetables
   until crisp-tender, about 4 minutes.
2. Add tuna, soy sauce, sugar, lemon juice and water. Stir-fry for
   1 minute.
3. Serve over hot rice.

Serves: 5   Serving size: ⅕ recipe

NUTRITION FACTS PER SERVING

Calories	254	*Carbohydrate choices*	2
Carbohydrate	28 g		
Protein	22 g	*Exchanges*	1½ starch
Fat	6 g		1 vegetable
Saturated fat	1 g		2 lean meat
Fiber	4 g		
Sodium	856 mg		

Albacore and Shells with Lemon Sauce ☺

1½ cups uncooked small pasta shells
1 can (6⅛ ounces) StarKist® Sold White Albacore in spring water, drained
1 tablespoon margarine or butter
½ cup chicken broth
¼ cup dry white wine
2 tablespoons lemon juice
1 tablespoon cornstarch
1 teaspoon lemon pepper seasoning, dried basil or dill weed
Salt and pepper to taste, optional
¼ teaspoon sugar
1 tablespoon finely chopped green onion

1. Cook pasta according to package directions. Drain and place in serving bowl. Mix in tuna.
2. In same pasta pot, melt margarine.
3. In small bowl, combine broth, wine, lemon juice, cornstarch and lemon pepper seasoning, stirring until cornstarch is dissolved. Add cornstarch mixture to melted margarine.
4. Bring sauce to a boil and boil 1 minute, stirring constantly. Season with salt and pepper, if desired; add sugar.
5. Pour sauce over tuna and pasta. Sprinkle with green onion.

Serves: 4   Serving size: ¼ recipe

NUTRITION FACTS PER SERVING

Calories	288	*Carbohydrate choices*	3
Carbohydrate	41 g		
Protein	18 g	*Exchanges*	3 starch
Fat	4 g		1 very lean meat
Saturated fat	1 g		
Fiber	2 g		
Sodium	398 mg		

Nutty Albacore Salad Pitas ◔

1 can (6⅛ ounces) StarKist® Solid White Albacore in spring water, drained
½ cup light mayonnaise
⅓ cup diced celery
¼ cup raisins or ½ cup grapes, halved
¼ cup chopped nuts (walnuts, pecans or almonds)
½ teaspoon dried dill weed, optional
Salt and pepper to taste, optional
2 whole wheat pita breads, halved
4 lettuce leaves

1. Combine tuna, mayonnaise, celery, raisins, nuts and dill weed, if
   desired. Season with salt and pepper, if desired.
2. Line bread halves with lettuce leaves. Divide tuna mixture among
   bread pockets and serve.

Serves: 4   Serving size: 1

NUTRITION FACTS PER SERVING

Calories	285	*Carbohydrate choices*	1½
Carbohydrate	24 g		
Protein	14 g	*Exchanges*	1½ starch
Fat	16 g		1 meat
Saturated fat	2 g		2 fat
Fiber	3 g		
Sodium	500 mg		

One-dish Meals

One-dish Chicken Bake

3 cups Stove Top® Stuffing Mix for Chicken
1¼ cups hot water
2 tablespoons margarine, cut up
4 boneless, skinless chicken-breast halves (about 1¼ pounds)
1 can (10¾ ounces) condensed cream of mushroom soup
⅓ cup skim milk

1. Preheat oven to 375° F. Stir stuffing mix, hot water and margarine just until moistened; set aside.
2. Place chicken in 12 x 8-inch baking dish. Mix soup and milk; pour over chicken.
3. Top with stuffing. Bake 35 minutes or until chicken is cooked through.

Serves: 4   Serving size: ¼ recipe

NUTRITION FACTS PER SERVING

Calories	440	*Carbohydrate choices* 3	
Carbohydrate	45 g		
Protein	30 g	*Exchanges*	3 starch
Fat	15 g		2 lean meat
Saturated fat	3 g		½ fat
Fiber	2 g		
Sodium	1475 mg		

Cheesy Chicken Casserole

$\frac{1}{2}$ cup Miracle Whip® Light® Salad Dressing
$1\frac{1}{2}$ cups (6 ounces) Kraft® Natural Shredded Reduced Fat Cheddar
    Cheese, divided
$1\frac{1}{2}$ cups chopped cooked chicken
$1\frac{1}{2}$ cups cooked rotini pasta
2 cups frozen mixed vegetables
$\frac{1}{4}$ cup skim milk
$\frac{1}{2}$ teaspoon dried basil

Oven Directions

1. Preheat oven to 350° F. Mix all ingredients except $\frac{1}{2}$ cup cheese. Spoon
   into $1\frac{1}{2}$-quart casserole.
2. Sprinkle with remaining $\frac{1}{2}$ cup cheese. Bake 30 minutes or until
   thoroughly heated.

Microwave Directions

1. Mix all ingredients except $\frac{1}{2}$ cup cheese. Spoon into $1\frac{1}{2}$-quart
   microwave-safe casserole.
2. Sprinkle with remaining $\frac{1}{2}$ cup cheese. Microwave on high 8 to 10
   minutes or until thoroughly heated.

Serves: 6   Serving size: $\frac{1}{6}$ recipe

NUTRITION FACTS PER SERVING

Calories	328	*Carbohydrate choices*	2
Carbohydrate	33 g		
Protein	24 g	*Exchanges*	2 starch
Fat	11 g		3 lean meat
Saturated fat	4 g		
Fiber	3 g		
Sodium	477 mg		

Campbell's® One-dish Chicken and Rice Bake

1 can (10³/₄ ounces) Campbell's® Condensed Cream of Mushroom Soup
1 cup water (for creamier rice, increase water to 1¹/₃ cups)
³/₄ cup uncooked regular white rice
¹/₄ teaspoon paprika
¹/₄ teaspoon pepper
4 boneless, skinless chicken-breast halves

1. Preheat oven to 375° F. In 2-quart shallow baking dish mix soup, water, rice, paprika and pepper.
2. Place chicken on rice mixture. Sprinkle with additional paprika and pepper, if desired. Cover.
3. Bake 45 minutes or until done.

Serves: 4   Serving size: ¹/₄ recipe

NUTRITION FACTS PER SERVING

Calories	339	*Carbohydrate choices* 2	
Carbohydrate	35 g		
Protein	29 g	*Exchanges*	2 starch
Fat	8 g		3 lean meat
Saturated fat	2 g		
Fiber	1 g		
Sodium	592 mg		

No-guilt Chicken Pot Pie

*1 can (10¾ ounces) Campbell's® Condensed 98% Fat Free Cream of
   Chicken Soup*
1 package (9 ounces) frozen mixed vegetables, thawed
1 cup cubed cooked chicken
½ cup skim milk
1 egg
1 cup Bisquick® Reduced Fat Baking Mix

1. Preheat oven to 400° F. In 9-inch pie plate mix soup, vegetables and
   chicken.
2. Mix milk, egg and baking mix in separate bowl. Pour over chicken
   mixture.
3. Bake 30 minutes or until golden.

Serves: 4   Serving size: ¼ pie

NUTRITION FACTS PER SERVING

Calories	268	*Carbohydrate choices*	2
Carbohydrate	32 g		
Protein	19 g	*Exchanges*	2 starch
Fat	7 g		1 vegetable
Saturated fat	2 g		2 lean meat
Fiber	2 g		
Sodium	1009 mg		

Shepherd's Pie

3 cups frozen peas and carrots
1 cup frozen chopped onion, thawed
1 cup frozen chopped green pepper, thawed
2 teaspoons dried thyme
2 teaspoons paprika
Vegetable cooking spray
4 cups refrigerated mashed potatoes
⅔ cup light ricotta cheese
2 cups canned black-eyed peas, drained
1 cup canned diced tomatoes
1 can (8 ounces) tomato sauce
2 teaspoons Worcestershire sauce
Paprika for garnish

1. Preheat oven to 400° F. Combine peas and carrots, onion, green pepper, thyme and paprika. Spoon into large oblong glass baking dish coated with cooking spray. Bake uncovered for 20 minutes, stirring halfway through baking time. Set aside.
2. Mix mashed potatoes and ricotta cheese. Set aside.
3. Combine baked vegetable mixture, black-eyed peas, tomatoes, tomato sauce and Worcestershire sauce, stirring well. Spoon into 2½-quart baking dish coated with cooking spray.
4. Spoon hash brown mixture in border around edge of dish; spoon remaining potatoes in center of dish. Sprinkle additional paprika over top. Reduce heat to 350° F and bake, uncovered, for 20 minutes.

Serves: 8   Serving size: ⅛ recipe

NUTRITION FACTS PER SERVING

Calories	219	*Carbohydrate choices*	3
Carbohydrate	42 g		
Protein	10 g	*Exchanges*	2½ starch
Fat	2 g		1 vegetable
Saturated fat	1 g		
Fiber	8 g		
Sodium	427 mg		

Turkey Cottage Pie

3 tablespoons margarine or butter
¼ cup all-purpose flour
1 envelope Lipton® Recipe Secrets® Golden Onion or Savory Herb with
    Garlic Soup Mix
2 cups water
2 cups diced cooked turkey or chicken
1 package (10 ounces) frozen mixed vegetables, thawed
1¼ cups shredded Swiss or cheddar cheese (about 5 ounces), divided
5 cups refrigerated mashed potatoes, cooked according to package directions

1. Preheat oven to 375° F. In large saucepan, melt margarine over medium
   heat; add flour and cook, stirring constantly, 5 minutes or until golden.
2. Combine soup mix with water and stir into flour mixture. Bring to a
   boil over high heat. Reduce heat to low and simmer 15 minutes or
   until thickened.
3. Stir in turkey, vegetables and 1 cup cheese. Spoon into lightly greased
   2-quart casserole; top with cooked potatoes, then remaining ¼ cup
   cheese.
4. Bake 30 minutes or until bubbling.

Serves: 8   Serving size: ⅛ recipe

NUTRITION FACTS PER SERVING

Calories	293	*Carbohydrate choices*	2
Carbohydrate	30 g		
Protein	19 g	*Exchanges*	2 starch
Fat	11 g		2 meat
Saturated fat	4 g		
Fiber	4 g		
Sodium	584 mg		

Couscous with
Turkey Pepperoni and Broccoli ☯

1 pound fresh broccoli, cut into florets
1 tablespoon minced garlic
½ teaspoon coarsely ground black pepper
1 tablespoon vegetable oil
1½ cups water
1 package (6.5 ounces) Marrakesh Express® Wild Mushroom Couscous
2 cups (6 ounces) Hormel® Turkey Pepperoni
¼ cup pitted kalamata olives, quartered

1. In large skillet over medium heat, cook broccoli, garlic, and black pepper in oil 5 to 6 minutes or until crisp-tender.
2. Add water and flavor packet from couscous; bring to a boil. Remove from heat.
3. Stir in couscous and pepperoni. Cover. Let stand 7 minutes. Sprinkle with olives.

Serves: 6   Serving size: ⅙ recipe

NUTRITION FACTS PER SERVING

Calories	217	Carbohydrate choices	1½
Carbohydrate	22 g		
Protein	15 g	Exchanges	1 starch
Fat	7 g		1 vegetable
Saturated fat	2 g		1 meat
Fiber	2 g		
Sodium	771 mg		

Seafood Casserole

Vegetable cooking spray
1 teaspoon vegetable oil
¾ pound sliced fresh mushrooms
2 cups frozen chopped green pepper
1 cup frozen chopped onion
1 teaspoon oregano
4 teaspoons minced garlic
1 cup spaghetti sauce
½ cup canned chicken broth, undiluted
½ cup dry white wine, optional
⅔ pound large sea scallops, cut in half
½ pound swordfish steak, cubed
3 cups cooked rice
⅓ cup grated Parmesan cheese

1. Preheat oven to 350° F. Coat large Dutch oven with cooking spray. Add oil and place over medium-high heat until hot. Add mushrooms, green pepper, onion, oregano and garlic. Sauté 10 minutes until onion is tender.
2. Stir in spaghetti sauce and broth and wine, if desired. Bring to a boil.
3. Stir in scallops and fish. Remove from heat and stir in rice.
4. Spoon mixture into 13 x 9 x 2-inch baking dish coated with cooking spray. Bake, uncovered, 30 minutes.
5. Stir, sprinkle with grated cheese, and bake 10 minutes longer or until cheese melts.

Serves: 6   Serving size: ⅙ recipe

NUTRITION FACTS PER SERVING

Calories	297	*Carbohydrate choices*	2½
Carbohydrate	36 g		
Protein	24 g	*Exchanges*	2 starch
Fat	7 g		1 vegetable
Saturated fat	2 g		2 lean meat
Fiber	3 g		
Sodium	896 mg		

Creamy Ham Casserole

2 cups fresh or frozen broccoli florets, thawed if frozen

1½ cups (6 ounces) Kraft® ⅓ Less Fat Natural Shredded Cheddar Cheese, divided

1½ cups coarsely chopped ham

3 cups cooked rotini pasta

½ cup Miracle Whip® Light® Salad Dressing

½ cup chopped green or red pepper

¼ cup skim milk

Seasoned croutons, optional

Oven Directions

1. Preheat oven to 350° F. Mix all ingredients except ½ cup of the cheese and the croutons. Spoon into 1½-quart casserole.
2. Sprinkle with remaining ½ cup cheese. Bake 30 minutes or until thoroughly heated.
3. Sprinkle with seasoned croutons, if desired.

Microwave Directions

1. Mix all ingredients except ½ cup of the cheese and the croutons. Spoon into 1½-quart microwave-safe casserole.
2. Microwave on high 8 to 10 minutes or until thoroughly heated. Sprinkle with seasoned croutons, if desired.

Serves: 8   Serving size: ⅛ recipe

NUTRITION FACTS PER SERVING

Calories	227	*Carbohydrate choices*	1
Carbohydrate	20 g		
Protein	15 g	*Exchanges*	1 starch
Fat	9 g		1 vegetable
Saturated fat	4 g		2 meat
Fiber	1 g		
Sodium	693 mg		

Beef and Couscous Skillet

1 pound lean boneless top sirloin steak, trimmed of visible fat and sliced
 into 1/4-inch wide strips
1/4 teaspoon pepper
Vegetable cooking spray
1 teaspoon vegetable oil
2 teaspoons minced garlic
2 cups frozen vegetable mix (broccoli, carrot and cauliflower), thawed
1 can (14 1/2 ounces) beef broth
1 cup uncooked couscous
1 1/2 cups chopped fresh tomato
1/2 cup chopped fresh basil
2 tablespoons balsamic or red wine vinegar

1. Sprinkle steak with pepper. Coat large skillet with cooking spray; place
   over medium-high heat and add meat, cooking 5 to 7 minutes until
   browned on all sides. Remove meat from skillet and keep warm.
2. Add oil to skillet. Add garlic and cook 30 seconds; add vegetable mix
   and broth. Bring to a boil; cover, reduce heat and simmer 4 minutes
   until vegetables are crisp-tender.
3. Stir in meat and couscous; cover and let stand 5 minutes or until liquid
   is absorbed.
4. Add tomato, basil and vinegar; stir well.

Serves: 4   Serving size: 1/4 recipe

NUTRITION FACTS PER SERVING

Calories	346	*Carbohydrate choices*	3
Carbohydrate	44 g		
Protein	31 g	*Exchanges*	2 1/2 starch
Fat	5 g		1 vegetable
Saturated fat	1 g		3 very lean meat
Fiber	5 g		
Sodium	538 mg		

Texas Hash

1 pound extra-lean ground beef
1 cup frozen chopped onion
1 cup frozen chopped green pepper
2 cups canned diced tomatoes, with juice
½ cup uncooked long-grain rice
2 teaspoons chili powder
½ teaspoon ground black pepper
6 ounces tomato juice

1. Preheat oven to 350° F. Brown ground beef in large skillet; drain. Remove meat and set aside.
2. Add onion and green pepper to skillet; sauté until tender.
3. Return beef to skillet and mix with vegetables. Add tomatoes, rice, chili powder and pepper; mix well.
4. Pour mixture into 2-quart baking dish. Cover and bake 45 minutes. Remove cover, stir in tomato juice, and bake uncovered 15 minutes longer.

Serves: 8   Serving size: 1 cup

NUTRITION FACTS PER SERVING

Calories	178	*Carbohydrate choices*	1
Carbohydrate	16 g		
Protein	13 g	*Exchanges*	1 starch
Fat	7 g		1 vegetable
Saturated fat	2 g		1 meat
Fiber	1 g		
Sodium	208 mg		

Family Spaghetti Pie

1 pound extra-lean ground beef
1 cup Pace® Picante Sauce
1 cup Prego® Spaghetti Sauce with Mushrooms
3 cups cooked spaghetti
⅓ cup grated Parmesan cheese
1 egg, beaten
1 tablespoon margarine or butter, melted
1 cup light ricotta cheese
1 cup shredded mozzarella cheese

1. Preheat oven to 350° F. In skillet over medium-high heat, cook ground beef until browned, stirring to separate meat; drain. Stir in picante sauce and spaghetti sauce. Heat through; set aside.
2. Mix spaghetti, Parmesan cheese, egg and margarine in separate bowl. Spread on bottom and sides of greased 10-inch pie plate. Spread ricotta cheese in spaghetti shell. Top with beef mixture.
3. Bake 30 minutes or until hot. Sprinkle with mozzarella cheese. Let stand 5 minutes. Cut into 6 wedges.

Serves: 6   Serving size: 1 wedge

NUTRITION FACTS PER SERVING

Calories	412	*Carbohydrate choices*	2
Carbohydrate	29 g		
Protein	33 g	*Exchanges*	2 starch
Fat	18 g		4 lean meat
Saturated fat	7 g		1 fat
Fiber	2 g		
Sodium	676 mg		

Mexican Lasagna

1 pound extra-lean ground beef
1 can (17 ounces) whole kernel corn, drained
1 cup salsa
1 can (15 ounces) tomato sauce
1 envelope taco seasoning mix
1 carton (16 ounces) low fat cottage cheese
2 eggs
1 teaspoon oregano
1 package (10 or 12) Azteca® Corn Tortillas
½ cup shredded reduced-fat cheddar cheese
½ cup shredded reduced-fat Monterey Jack cheese

1. Preheat oven to 375° F. Brown ground beef and drain. Add corn, salsa, tomato sauce and seasoning mix. Simmer, stirring frequently for 5 minutes.
2. In separate bowl, combine cottage cheese, eggs and oregano.
3. Line bottom of a greased 13 x 9-inch baking dish with 5 or 6 tortillas, overlapping edges. Top with half the meat mixture. Spoon cottage cheese mixture over meat. Arrange remaining 5 or 6 tortillas over cheese mixture. Spread remaining meat mixture over all and top with shredded cheeses.
4. Bake for 30 minutes or until the cheese is melted and casserole bubbles. Let stand 10 minutes before serving.

Serves: 8   Serving size: ⅛ recipe

NUTRITION FACTS PER SERVING

Calories 354
Carbohydrate 36 g
Protein 28 g
Fat 12 g
Saturated fat 5 g
Fiber 5 g
Sodium 1183 mg

Carbohydrate choices 2½

Exchanges 2½ starch
3 lean meat

Chunky Chili Casserole

2 cups Stove Top® Chicken Flavor or Cornbread Stuffing Mix
½ cup hot water
½ pound extra-lean ground beef
1 small onion, chopped
1 can (15 ounces) chili with beans
1½ cups (6 ounces) Kraft® Natural Shredded Reduced Fat Cheddar
    Cheese, divided
½ cup frozen sweet corn, thawed
¼ cup sliced pitted ripe olives
Light sour cream, optional

Microwave Directions

1. Mix stuffing mix and hot water in 2-quart microwave-safe casserole.
   Spread evenly in casserole.
2. Mix ground beef and onion in large microwave-safe bowl. Cover
   loosely with wax paper. Microwave on high 4 minutes or until meat is
   no longer pink; drain.
3. Mix meat with chili, 1 cup cheese, corn and olives. Spoon over stuffing.
4. Cover casserole loosely with wax paper. Microwave 10 minutes, rotat-
   ing halfway through cooking time. Let stand 5 minutes.
5. Sprinkle with remaining ½ cup cheese. Serve with sour cream, if
   desired.

Serves: 6   Serving size: ⅙ recipe

NUTRITION FACTS PER SERVING

Calories	358	*Carbohydrate choices*	2
Carbohydrate	31 g		
Protein	23 g	*Exchanges*	2 starch
Fat	16 g		2 meat
Saturated fat	7 g		1 fat
Fiber	3 g		
Sodium	919 mg		

Picadillo Chili ⊙

1 can (15 ounces) Hormel® Chili No Beans
1 can (10 ounces) Chi-Chi's® Diced Tomatoes with Green Chilies
1 can (8 ounces) pineapple tidbits packaged in juice, undrained
$\frac{1}{2}$ cup raisins
$\frac{1}{4}$ cup slivered almonds, toasted
$\frac{1}{2}$ teaspoon chili powder
$\frac{1}{4}$ teaspoon ground cinnamon
2 cups cooked rice

1. In large saucepan over medium heat, combine all ingredients except rice. Bring to a boil. Reduce heat and simmer 10 minutes.
2. Serve over hot rice.

Serves: 6   Serving size: $\frac{1}{6}$ recipe

NUTRITION FACTS PER SERVING

Calories	290	*Carbohydrate choices* 2½	
Carbohydrate	39 g		
Protein	9 g	*Exchanges*	1½ starch
Fat	12 g		1 fruit
Saturated fat	4 g		1 meat
Fiber	2 g		1 fat
Sodium	565 mg		

Velveeta® Salsa Mac 'N Cheese ℚ

1 pound extra-lean ground beef
1 jar (16 ounces) chunky salsa
1¾ cups water
2 cups uncooked elbow macaroni
¾ pound (12 ounces) Velveeta® Process Cheese Spread, cut up

1. Brown ground beef in large skillet; drain. Add salsa and water. Bring to a boil.
2. Stir in macaroni. Reduce heat to medium-low; cover with tight fitting lid. Simmer 8 to 10 minutes or until macaroni is tender.
3. Add Velveeta®; stir until melted.

Serves: 8   Serving size: ⅛ recipe

NUTRITION FACTS PER SERVING

Calories	375	*Carbohydrate choices*	2
Carbohydrate	31 g		
Protein	24 g	*Exchanges*	2 starch
Fat	17 g		3 meat
Saturated fat	9 g		
Fiber	2 g		
Sodium	859 mg		

Meatless Entrees

Note: Meat exchanges in this chapter come from cheese and/or beans.

Baked Potatoes with Chili Topping

4 baking potatoes, scrubbed
1 can (15 ounces) chili
2 tablespoons Velveeta® Shredded Pasteurized Process Cheese Food

Potato Microwave Directions

1. Pierce potatoes; place on paper towel in microwave. Microwave on high 16 to 20 minutes or until tender, turning potatoes over and rearranging after 10 minutes.
2. Let stand 5 minutes. Split potatoes; fluff with fork.

Topping Microwave Directions

1. Place chili in medium microwave-safe bowl; cover loosely. Microwave on high 3 to 4 minutes or until thoroughly heated.
2. Spoon chili over potatoes. Sprinkle with shredded Velveeta®.

Serves: 4   Serving size: 1 potato

NUTRITION FACTS PER SERVING

Calories	259	*Carbohydrate choices*	2
Carbohydrate	34 g		
Protein	11 g	*Exchanges*	2 starch
Fat	9 g		1 meat
Saturated fat	4 g		
Fiber	4 g		
Sodium	630 mg		

Baked Potatoes
with Cheesy Greek Topping

4 baking potatoes, scrubbed
½ pound torn spinach
1 cup sliced mushrooms
2 tablespoons Seven Seas® Viva Herbs & Spices Dressing
1 cup (4 ounces) Kraft® Natural Shredded Low-Moisture Part-Skim
     Mozzarella Cheese
¼ cup sliced pitted ripe olives
¼ cup Kraft® 100% Grated Parmesan Cheese

Potato Microwave Directions

1. Pierce potatoes; place on paper towel in microwave. Microwave on
   high 16 to 20 minutes or until tender, turning potatoes over and
   rearranging after 10 minutes.
2. Let stand 5 minutes. Split potatoes; fluff with fork.

Topping Microwave Directions

1. Mix spinach, mushrooms and dressing in 2-quart microwave-safe
   bowl; cover loosely.
2. Microwave on high 2 to 3 minutes or until spinach is limp. Stir in mozzarella cheese and olives.
3. Spoon over potatoes. Sprinkle with Parmesan cheese, 1 tablespoon per
   potato.

Serves: 4   Serving size: 1 potato

NUTRITION FACTS PER SERVING

Calories	237	*Carbohydrate choices*	2
Carbohydrate	27 g		
Protein	12 g	*Exchanges*	1½ starch
Fat	9 g		1 vegetable
Saturated fat	3 g		1 meat
Fiber	3 g		½ fat
Sodium	516 mg		

Southwestern Baked Potatoes

4 medium hot baked potatoes, split
1 cup shredded reduced-fat cheddar cheese
1 cup Pace® Picante Sauce
¹/₄ cup sliced pitted ripe olives
¹/₄ cup crumbled tortilla chips

Microwave Directions

1. Pierce potatoes; place on paper towel in microwave. Microwave on high 16 to 20 minutes or until tender, turning potatoes over and rearranging after 10 minutes.
2. Let stand 5 minutes. Split potatoes; fluff with fork.
3. Top each potato with cheese, picante sauce, olives and chips.

Serves: 4   Serving size: 1 potato

NUTRITION FACTS PER SERVING

Calories	214	*Carbohydrate choices*	2
Carbohydrate	28 g		
Protein	11 g	*Exchanges*	2 starch
Fat	7 g		1 meat
Saturated fat	3 g		
Fiber	3 g		
Sodium	448 mg		

Pizza Quesadillas ⊘

1 package (10 tortillas) Buena Vida™ Fat Free Flour Tortillas
1 cup pizza sauce
1 cup chopped green pepper
1 cup sliced fresh mushrooms
¼ cup grated Parmesan cheese
1½ cups shredded part-skim mozzarella cheese
Vegetable cooking spray

1. Remove tortillas from refrigerator; set aside. Preheat oven to 350° F.
   Heat tortillas according to package directions.
2. Spread approximately 1½ tablespoons pizza sauce on upper half of
   tortilla. Top with one-tenth of the green pepper, mushrooms, Parmesan
   cheese and mozzarella cheese. Fold bottom of tortilla over ingredients
   to form a half moon shape. Repeat for all tortillas.
3. Place on baking sheet that has been lightly coated with cooking spray.
   Bake for 10 to 12 minutes or until tortillas are golden and the cheese
   is melted. Cut each tortilla in half to make 2 pieces each. Makes 20
   quesadillas.

Serves: 10   Serving size: 2 quesadillas

NUTRITION FACTS PER SERVING

Calories	153	*Carbohydrate choices*	1
Carbohydrate	16 g		
Protein	8 g	*Exchanges*	1 starch
Fat	6 g		1 meat
Saturated fat	3 g		
Fiber	1 g		
Sodium	350 mg		

Vegetable Pizza ☺

*2 cups frozen Birds Eye® Farm Fresh Mixtures Broccoli, Red Peppers,
Onions and Mushrooms*
1 12-inch pizza crust, Italian bread shell or foccacia
1 cup shredded part-skim mozzarella cheese, divided
Dried oregano, basil or Italian seasoning

1. Preheat oven according to directions on pizza crust package. Rinse vegetables in colander under warm water. Drain well; pat with paper towel to remove excess moisture.
2. Spread crust with vegetables and half the cheese. Sprinkle with herbs; top with remaining cheese.
3. Follow baking directions on pizza crust package; bake until hot and bubbly. Cut into 8 slices.

Serves: 8   Serving size: 1 slice

NUTRITION FACTS PER SERVING

Calories	262	*Carbohydrate choices* 2½	
Carbohydrate	36 g		
Protein	10 g	*Exchanges*	2½ starch
Fat	9 g		1 meat
Saturated fat	2 g		
Fiber	2 g		
Sodium	667 mg		

Chili Bean Pasta ☺

1 package (16 ounces) frozen Freshlike® Chili Bean Stir Fry
2 tablespoons water
1 jar (14 ounces) spaghetti sauce
2 cups cooked pasta
¼ cup grated Parmesan cheese

1. In large skillet, combine frozen chili bean stir fry and water. Cover and cook 7 to 10 minutes.
2. Uncover, add spaghetti sauce and heat through.
3. Serve over hot pasta or rice. Top each serving with 1 tablespoon Parmesan cheese.

Serves: 4   Serving size: ¼ recipe

NUTRITION FACTS PER SERVING

Calories	288	*Carbohydrate choices*	2
Carbohydrate	32 g		
Protein	18 g	*Exchanges*	2 starch
Fat	10 g		1 vegetable
Saturated fat	5 g		1 meat
Fiber	6 g		½ fat
Sodium	1156 mg		

Spinach Lasagna

1 container (16 ounces) Light n'Lively® Lowfat Cottage Cheese or Fat Free
  Cottage Cheese
1 package (10 ounces) frozen chopped spinach, thawed and well-drained
3 cups (12 ounces) Kraft® ⅓ Less Fat Shredded Low-Moisture Part Skim
  Mozzarella Cheese, divided
¾ cup (3 ounces) Kraft® 100% Grated Parmesan Cheese, divided
2 eggs, beaten
1 jar (28 ounces) spaghetti sauce, divided
9 lasagna noodles, cooked and drained
Fresh oregano, optional

1. Preheat oven to 350° F. Mix cottage cheese, spinach, 2 cups of the mozzarella cheese, ½ cup of the Parmesan cheese and eggs.
2. Layer 1 cup of the spaghetti sauce, 3 lasagna noodles and ½ of the cottage cheese mixture in 13 x 9-inch baking dish. Repeat layers. Top with remaining 3 noodles, 1 cup sauce, 1 cup mozzarella cheese and ¼ cup Parmesan cheese.
3. Bake 45 minutes. Let stand 10 minutes before serving. Garnish with fresh oregano, if desired.

Serves: 10   Serving size: ¹⁄₁₀ recipe

NUTRITION FACTS PER SERVING

Calories	299	*Carbohydrate choices*	1½
Carbohydrate	25 g		
Protein	23 g	*Exchanges*	1½ starch
Fat	13 g		3 lean meat
Saturated fat	6 g		½ fat
Fiber	2 g		
Sodium	1111 mg		

Pasta Primavera

1 can (10¾ ounces) Campbell's® Healthy Request Creative Chef™
    Condensed Cream of Mushroom with Roasted Garlic & Herbs Soup
½ cup skim milk
3 tablespoons grated Parmesan cheese
1 tablespoon lemon juice
⅛ teaspoon pepper
3 cups fresh-cut or frozen mixed vegetables
2 cups cooked spaghetti

1. In large nonstick skillet mix soup, milk, cheese, lemon juice and
   pepper. Bring to a boil over medium heat.
2. Add vegetables. Cover and cook over low heat 15 minutes or until vegetables are tender, stirring occasionally. Toss with spaghetti and serve
   immediately.

Serves: 4   *Serving size: ¼ recipe*

Tip

A combination of broccoli florets, cauliflower florets, and green or red
pepper strips works well with this recipe.

NUTRITION FACTS PER SERVING

Calories	199	*Carbohydrate choices* 2	
Carbohydrate	34 g		
Protein	9 g	*Exchanges*	2 starch
Fat	4 g		1 vegetable
Saturated fat	1 g		
Fiber	5 g		
Sodium	510 mg		

Cheesy Baked Ziti

¾ *pound ziti or rotelle pasta*
1 package (10 ounces) frozen broccoli florets
1 package (10 ounces) frozen cauliflower florets
1 container (15 ounces) nonfat ricotta cheese
1 cup shredded part-skim mozzarella cheese
¾ *teaspoon dried leaf oregano*
6 drops hot pepper sauce
1 jar (15 ounces) spaghetti sauce, divided
Grated Parmesan cheese, optional

1. Preheat oven to 450° F. Cook pasta in boiling water for 6 minutes. Add broccoli and cauliflower; cook pasta mixture for 2 minutes. Drain.
2. Combine ricotta, mozzarella, oregano, and hot pepper sauce in large bowl.
3. Toss pasta mixture with 1 cup spaghetti sauce. Spoon half of pasta mixture into 13 x 9 x 2-inch casserole dish (or individual casseroles). Spoon ⅔ of cheese mixture over top. Add remaining pasta, spoon on remaining sauce and top with remaining cheese mixture.
4. Bake, covered, for 25 minutes or until heated through. Serve with grated Parmesan cheese, if desired.

Serves: 8   Serving size: ⅛ *recipe*

NUTRITION FACTS PER SERVING

Calories	306	*Carbohydrate choices*	3
Carbohydrate	46 g		
Protein	19 g	*Exchanges*	3 starch
Fat	6 g		1 vegetable
Saturated fat	2 g		1 lean meat
Fiber	4 g		
Sodium	495 mg		

No-fuss Stuffed Shells

1 package (12 ounces) Creamette® Jumbo Stuffing Shells, uncooked
1 container (15 ounces) light ricotta cheese
1 egg, beaten
½ cup grated Parmesan cheese
½ teaspoon salt
½ teaspoon pepper
½ cup frozen spinach, thawed with excess water squeezed out
1 jar (26 ounces) Classico® DiParma Four Cheese Pasta Sauce
1 cup (4 ounces) shredded mozzarella cheese

1. Preheat oven to 350° F. Prepare stuffing shells according to package directions; drain.
2. Whip together ricotta cheese, egg, Parmesan cheese, salt and pepper. Stir in spinach.
3. Fill shells equally with cheese mixture. Pour half of the pasta sauce in a 9 x 13-inch baking dish, arrange shells on sauce, pour remaining sauce over shells.
4. Cover; bake 25 minutes. Uncover and top with mozzarella cheese. Return to oven for 5 minutes to melt cheese. Serve.

Serves: 8   Serving size: ⅛ recipe

Tip

To prepare this recipe ahead of time, prepare and fill shells as above. Place shells on baking sheet and freeze. Once frozen, individually wrap in plastic wrap and place in freezer bag. To prepare, just thaw, add sauce, and heat as above.

NUTRITION FACTS PER SERVING

Calories	347	Carbohydrate choices	3
Carbohydrate	44 g		
Protein	22 g	Exchanges	3 starch
Fat	8 g		2 lean meat
Saturated fat	4 g		
Fiber	2 g		
Sodium	641 mg		

Broccoli Pepper Macaroni ☺

1 package (7.25 ounces) Kraft® Thick 'N Creamy Macaroni and Cheese
1 cup frozen chopped broccoli, cooked and drained
¼ cup chopped red pepper
¼ cup chopped green pepper
⅛ teaspoon dill weed, optional

1. Prepare macaroni and cheese as directed on package, omitting margarine and using ½ cup skim milk instead.
2. Stir in remaining ingredients.

Serves: 4   Serving size: ¼ recipe

NUTRITION FACTS PER SERVING

Calories	204	*Carbohydrate choices*	2½
Carbohydrate	38 g		
Protein	9 g	*Exchanges*	2½ starch
Fat	2 g		
Saturated fat	1 g		
Fiber	2 g		
Sodium	425 mg		

Vegetarian Chili Mac ☉

1 package (7.25 ounces) Kraft® Macaroni & Cheese Original Flavor
1 cup canned kidney beans, rinsed and drained
1 cup chopped canned tomatoes
1 teaspoon chili powder

1. Prepare macaroni and cheese as directed on package.
2. Stir in remaining ingredients and serve.

Serves: 4   Serving size: ¼ recipe

NUTRITION FACTS PER SERVING

Calories	264	Carbohydrate choices	3
Carbohydrate	48 g		
Protein	13 g	Exchanges	3 starch
Fat	2 g		1 very lean meat
Saturated fat	1 g		
Fiber	4 g		
Sodium	737 mg		

Southwestern Vegetarian Chili ◔

2 cans (15 ounces each) chunky chili tomato sauce
1 bag (16 ounces) frozen Birds Eye® Farm Fresh Mixtures Broccoli, Corn
   and Red Peppers
1 can (15½ ounces) red kidney beans
1 can (1½ ounces) chopped green chiles
½ cup shredded reduced-fat cheddar cheese

1. Combine tomato sauce, vegetables, beans and chiles in large saucepan;
   bring to a boil.
2. Cook, uncovered, over medium heat 5 minutes.
3. Spoon into serving bowls and sprinkle each serving with cheese.

Serves: 8   Serving size: ⅛ recipe

NUTRITION FACTS PER SERVING

Calories	150	*Carbohydrate choices*	1
Carbohydrate	19 g		
Protein	8 g	*Exchanges*	1 starch
Fat	6 g		1 vegetable
Saturated fat	1 g		1 fat
Fiber	5 g		
Sodium	767 mg		

Hearty Meatless Chili

1 envelope Lipton® Recipe Secrets® Onion or Onion-Mushroom Soup Mix
4 cups water
1 can (16 ounces) chickpeas or garbanzo beans, rinsed and drained
1 can (16 ounces) red kidney beans, rinsed and drained
1 can (14½ ounces) whole peeled tomatoes, undrained and chopped
1 cup lentils, rinsed and drained
1 large rib celery, coarsely chopped
1 tablespoon chili powder
1 medium clove garlic, finely chopped
2 teaspoons ground cumin, optional
¼ teaspoon crushed red pepper flakes, optional

1. In 4-quart saucepan or stockpot, combine all ingredients. Bring to a
   boil over high heat. Reduce heat to low and simmer covered, stirring
   occasionally, 20 minutes or until lentils are almost tender.
2. Remove cover and simmer, stirring occasionally, an additional
   20 minutes or until liquid is almost absorbed and lentils are tender.

Serves: 8   Serving size: 1 cup

Serving Suggestion
Serve over hot rice and top with shredded reduced-fat cheddar cheese.

NUTRITION FACTS PER SERVING

Calories	217	*Carbohydrate choices* 2½	
Carbohydrate	38 g		
Protein	14 g	*Exchanges*	2½ starch
Fat	2 g		1 very lean meat
Saturated fat	<1 g		
Fiber	11 g		
Sodium	811 mg		

Tex-Mex Tortas

4 Buena Vida™ Fat Free Flour Tortillas
Vegetable cooking spray
1 cup fat-free refried beans
1 can (4 ounces) chopped green chiles, undrained
1 cup chopped tomato
1 cup salsa
6 ounces (1½ cups) shredded reduced-fat cheddar cheese
¼ cup sliced ripe olives

1. Preheat oven to 350° F. Remove tortillas from refrigerator; set aside. Spray a 9 x 1¼-inch pie pan with cooking spray.
2. Mix together beans, chiles and tomato. Place 1 tortilla in pie pan. Spread with ¼ bean mixture. Top with ¼ salsa and ¼ of shredded cheese and repeat 3 times. Top last layer with sliced black olives.
3. Cover loosely with foil. Bake 25 to 30 minutes until heated through and cheese is melted. Cut into 4 wedges.

Serves: 4   Serving size: 1 wedge

NUTRITION FACTS PER SERVING

Calories	288	*Carbohydrate choices*	2
Carbohydrate	32 g		
Protein	18 g	*Exchanges*	2 starch
Fat	10 g		1 vegetable
Saturated fat	5 g		1 meat
Fiber	6 g		½ fat
Sodium	1156 mg		

Black Bean Tacos ☺

1 carton (11 ounces) Morningstar Farms® Spicy Black Bean Burger
8 taco shells
½ cup shredded reduced-fat cheddar cheese
½ cup salsa
Lettuce, shredded

1. Preheat oven to 350° F. Defrost burgers in microwave oven or thaw at room temperature. Cut burgers in half.
2. Place 1 burger half in each taco shell. Place on baking sheet and bake 15 minutes.
3. Top each taco with shredded cheese, salsa and shredded lettuce.

Serves: 8   Serving size: 1 taco

NUTRITION FACTS PER SERVING

Calories	139	*Carbohydrate choices*	1
Carbohydrate	17 g		
Protein	9 g	*Exchanges*	1 starch
Fat	5 g		1 lean meat
Saturated fat	1 g		
Fiber	4 g		
Sodium	362 mg		

Breads, Side Dishes and Vegetables

Savory Rosemary Quick Bread

Vegetable cooking spray
1¾ cups reduced-fat all-purpose baking mix
1 cup (4 ounces) shredded cheddar cheese, divided
¾ cup skim milk
2 egg whites
1 can (2.8 ounces) French's® French Fried Onions, divided
1 tablespoon sugar
1 tablespoon margarine or butter, melted
2 teaspoons chopped fresh rosemary or ½ teaspoon dried rosemary

1. Preheat oven to 375° F. Line 9-inch square baking pan with foil; spray with cooking spray.
2. Combine baking mix, ½ cup cheese, milk, egg whites, ⅔ cup onions, sugar, margarine and rosemary in large bowl; stir just until moistened. Do not overmix. Spread into prepared pan. Bake 20 minutes or until toothpick inserted in center comes out clean.
3. Sprinkle with remaining cheese and onions. Bake 1 minute or until cheese is melted and onions are golden. Remove to wire rack; cool 5 minutes. Remove foil. Cut into squares. Serve warm or cool.

Serves: 8   Serving size: ⅛ recipe

NUTRITION FACTS PER SERVING

Calories	228	*Carbohydrate choices*	1½
Carbohydrate	25 g		
Protein	8 g	*Exchanges*	1½ starch
Fat	10 g		2 fat
Saturated fat	3 g		
Fiber	1 g		
Sodium	486 mg		

Crispy Onion Crescent Rolls

1 can (8 ounces) refrigerated crescent dinner rolls
1 can (2.8 ounces) French's® French Fried Onions, slightly crushed
1 egg, beaten

1. Preheat oven to 375° F. Line large baking sheet with foil. Separate refrigerated rolls into 8 triangles.
2. Sprinkle center of each triangle with about 1½ tablespoons onions. Roll up triangles from short side, jelly-roll fashion. Arrange crescents on prepared baking sheet.
3. Brush with beaten egg. Sprinkle any excess onions over top of crescents.
4. Bake 15 minutes or until golden brown and crispy. Transfer to wire rack; cool slightly.

Serves: 8   Serving size: 1 roll

NUTRITION FACTS PER SERVING

Calories	166	*Carbohydrate choices*	1
Carbohydrate	17 g		
Protein	3 g	*Exchanges*	1 starch
Fat	9 g		2 fat
Saturated fat	2 g		
Fiber	1 g		
Sodium	414 mg		

Broccoli and Cheddar Muffins

3 cups all-purpose baking mix
2 eggs, lightly beaten
⅔ cup skim milk
1 teaspoon dried basil
1 cup reduced-fat shredded cheddar cheese
1 box (10 ounces) frozen Birds Eye® Chopped Broccoli
Vegetable cooking spray

1. Preheat oven to 350° F. Combine baking mix, eggs, milk and basil. Mix until moistened (do not overmix). Add cheese and broccoli; stir just to combine.
2. Spray 12 muffin cups with cooking spray. Pour batter into muffin cups. Bake 25 to 30 minutes or until golden brown. Cool 5 minutes in pan. Loosen sides of muffins with knife; remove from pan and serve warm.

Serves: 12   Serving size: 1 muffin

NUTRITION FACTS PER SERVING

Calories	176	*Carbohydrate choices*	1½
Carbohydrate	21 g		
Protein	7 g	*Exchanges*	1½ starch
Fat	7 g		1 fat
Saturated fat	2 g		
Fiber	1 g		
Sodium	439 mg		

Zesty Bruschetta ☺

1 envelope Lipton® Recipe Secrets® Savory Herb with Garlic or Italian
  Herb with Tomato Soup Mix
3 tablespoons olive or vegetable oil
1 loaf French or Italian bread (about 18 inches long), halved lengthwise
2 tablespoons shredded or grated Parmesan cheese

1. Preheat oven to 350° F. Blend soup mix and oil. Brush onto bread
   halves, then sprinkle with cheese.
2. Bake cut side up on baking sheet 15 minutes. Slice and serve.

Serves: 18   Serving size: 1 slice

NUTRITION FACTS PER SERVING

Calories	97	*Carbohydrate choices*	1
Carbohydrate	14 g		
Protein	3 g	*Exchanges*	1 starch
Fat	3 g		
Saturated fat	1 g		
Fiber	1 g		
Sodium	352 mg		

Creamy Vegetables ☻

*1 can (10¾ ounces) Campbell's® Healthy Request® Condensed Cream of
    Mushroom Soup*
½ cup skim milk
¼ teaspoon dried basil, crushed
⅛ teaspoon pepper
1 bag (16 ounces) frozen vegetable mix (broccoli, cauliflower and carrots)
1 can (8 ounces) sliced mushrooms, drained

1. In 10-inch skillet over medium heat, combine soup, milk, basil and
   pepper. Heat to boiling, stirring occasionally.
2. Add frozen vegetables and mushrooms, return to boiling. Reduce heat
   to low Cover; cook 10 minutes or until vegetables are tender, stirring
   occasionally.

Serves: 8   Serving size: ⅛ recipe

NUTRITION FACTS PER SERVING

Calories	47	*Carbohydrate choices* ½	
Carbohydrate	8 g		
Protein	3 g	*Exchanges* ½ starch or 2 vegetable	
Fat	1 g		
Saturated fat	<1 g		
Fiber	2 g		
Sodium	280 mg		

Broccoli-Carrot Bake

Vegetable cooking spray
2 cups Kellogg's® Product 19® cereal, crushed to 1 cup
2 teaspoons margarine, melted
2 packages (10 ounces each) frozen chopped broccoli, thawed and drained
1 cup frozen carrots, thawed and drained
1 can (10¾ ounces) condensed cream of mushroom soup
½ cup skim milk
Paprika

1. Preheat oven to 375° F. Coat 2-quart glass baking dish with cooking spray. Set aside.
2. In small bowl, combine cereal and margarine. Set aside for topping.
3. Spread vegetables in prepared baking dish. In small bowl, stir together soup and milk. Pour over vegetables. Sprinkle evenly with topping and paprika.
4. Bake about 30 minutes or until thoroughly heated. Serve warm.

Serves: 8   Serving size: ⅛ recipe

NUTRITION FACTS PER SERVING

Calories	102	*Carbohydrate choices*	1
Carbohydrate	15 g		
Protein	4 g	*Exchanges*	½ starch
Fat	4 g		1 vegetable
Saturated fat	1 g		½ fat
Fiber	3 g		
Sodium	389 mg		

Baked Spiced Squash

2 boxes (12 ounces each) frozen Birds Eye® Cooked Winter Squash, thawed
2 egg whites, lightly beaten
¼ cup brown sugar
2 teaspoons margarine or butter, melted
1 teaspoon cinnamon
Vegetable cooking spray
½ cup herbed croutons, coarsely crushed

1. Preheat oven to 400° F. Combine squash, egg whites, brown sugar, margarine and cinnamon; mix well. Pour into 1-quart baking dish sprayed with cooking spray.
2. Bake for 20 to 25 minutes or until center is set. Remove from oven; sprinkle crushed croutons on top. Bake 5 to 7 minutes longer or until croutons are browned.

Serves: 8   Serving size: ⅛ recipe

NUTRITION FACTS PER SERVING

Calories	93	*Carbohydrate choices*	1½
Carbohydrate	21 g		
Protein	2 g	*Exchanges*	1½ starch
Fat	1 g		
Saturated fat	<1 g		
Fiber	3 g		
Sodium	44 mg		

Green Bean Bake

1 can (10¾ ounces) Campbell's® Reduced Fat Condensed Cream of Mushroom Soup

½ cup skim milk

1 teaspoon soy sauce

Dash pepper

4 cups cooked cut green beans or frozen French-cut green beans, thawed and drained

1 can (2.8 ounces) French's® French Fried Onions, divided

1. Preheat oven to 350° F. In 1½-quart casserole, mix soup, milk, soy sauce, pepper, green beans and ½ can onions.
2. Bake 25 minutes or until hot.
3. Stir. Sprinkle remaining onions over bean mixture. Bake 5 minutes longer or until onions are golden.

Serves: 6   Serving size: ⅙ recipe

NUTRITION FACTS PER SERVING

Calories	144	*Carbohydrate choices*	1
Carbohydrate	16 g		
Protein	4 g	*Exchanges*	1 starch
Fat	8 g		1 vegetable
Saturated fat	1 g		1 fat
Fiber	3 g		
Sodium	556 mg		

Zesty Roasted Potato Salad

1 package (2.9 ounces) Shake 'N Bake® Perfect Potatoes Seasoning Mix for Fresh Potatoes, Herb & Garlic Flavor
8 medium potatoes (about 2½ pounds)
⅓ cup Kraft® Free® Italian Fat Free Dressing
¼ cup Kraft® 100% Grated Parmesan Cheese
¼ cup chopped fresh parsley
¼ cup chopped roasted red pepper

1. Prepare 2 batches Perfect Potatoes as directed on package, using both envelopes.
2. Remove from oven; spoon hot potatoes into large bowl.
3. Add remaining ingredients; toss lightly. Serve warm or at room temperature.

Serves: 10   Serving size: ¹⁄₁₀ recipe

NUTRITION FACTS PER SERVING

Calories	142	*Carbohydrate choices*	2
Carbohydrate	30 g		
Protein	4 g	*Exchanges*	2 starch
Fat	1 g		
Saturated fat	1 g		
Fiber	3 g		
Sodium	821 mg		

Spanish-style Rice

1 tablespoon vegetable oil
1 cup uncooked regular long-grain white rice
1 can (10½ ounces) Campbell's® Condensed Chicken Broth
1 cup water
½ cup Pace® Picante Sauce
½ teaspoon ground cumin
¼ teaspoon garlic powder
1 medium tomato, chopped
1 cup frozen peas

1. In skillet over medium heat, heat oil. Add rice and cook until browned, stirring constantly.
2. Stir in broth, water, picante sauce, cumin and garlic powder. Heat to a boil. Cover and cook over low heat 15 minutes.
3. Add tomato and peas; cook 5 minutes or until rice is done.

Serves: 6   Serving size: ⅙ recipe

NUTRITION FACTS PER SERVING

Calories	184	*Carbohydrate choices* 2
Carbohydrate	32 g	
Protein	6 g	*Exchanges* 2 starch
Fat	3 g	
Saturated fat	<1 g	
Fiber	2 g	
Sodium	390 mg	

Quick Mushroom Risotto ◷

1 can (13¾ ounces) chicken broth
½ cup water
1 jar (4 ounces) sliced mushrooms, drained
1 tablespoon margarine or butter, optional
½ teaspoon dried basil
¼ teaspoon garlic powder
2 cups uncooked Minute® Original Rice
¾ cup Kraft® Free® Nonfat Grated Topping

1. Bring broth, water, mushrooms, margarine, basil and garlic powder to a boil in medium saucepan.
2. Stir in rice and grated topping; cover. Remove from heat. Let stand 5 minutes. Fluff with fork.

Serves: 6   Serving size: ⅙ recipe

NUTRITION FACTS PER SERVING

Calories	204	*Carbohydrate choices*	3
Carbohydrate	41 g		
Protein	6 g	*Exchanges*	3 starch
Fat	1 g		
Saturated fat	<1 g		
Fiber	1 g		
Sodium	598 mg		

Caribbean Peas and Rice ⊙

2 slices bacon, cut into 1-inch pieces
1 cup frozen Birds Eye® Green Peas
1 cup uncooked instant rice
²/₃ cup water
¼ cup orange juice
½ teaspoon dried thyme leaves
Salt and pepper to taste, optional

1. Cook bacon in medium skillet over medium-high heat until golden brown; drain.
2. Add remaining ingredients and cook 5 to 7 minutes or until rice is tender and heated through, stirring occasionally. Season with salt and pepper, if desired. Serve hot.

Serves: 4   Serving size: ¼ recipe

NUTRITION FACTS PER SERVING

Calories	158	*Carbohydrate choices*	2
Carbohydrate	30 g		
Protein	5 g	*Exchanges*	2 starch
Fat	2 g		
Saturated fat	1 g		
Fiber	2 g		
Sodium	79 mg		

Easy Spanish Rice ☺

1 jar (16 ounces) salsa
¾ cup water
1½ cups uncooked instant rice
1 tablespoon margarine or butter

1. In medium saucepan, stir together the salsa and water. Bring to a boil.
2. Remove pan from heat; stir in rice and margarine.
3. Cover pan and let sit for 5 minutes. Stir with a fork before serving.

Serves: 6   Serving size: ⅙ recipe

NUTRITION FACTS PER SERVING

Calories	141	*Carbohydrate choices*	2
Carbohydrate	27 g		
Protein	3 g	*Exchanges*	2 starch
Fat	2 g		
Saturated fat	<1 g		
Fiber	2 g		
Sodium	222 mg		

Presto Primavera ☺

1½ *cups uncooked pasta (penne, spirals or macaroni)*
1 *can (8.5 ounces) Del Monte® FreshCut™ Sweet Peas, drained*
1 *can (8 ounces) Del Monte® Freshcut™ Green Beans, drained*
1 *can (8.25 ounces) Del Monte® FreshCut™ Sliced Carrots, drained*
1 *can (14.5 ounces) Del Monte® FreshCut™ Diced Tomatoes with*
Garlic & Onion
Salt and pepper to taste, optional
Grated Parmesan cheese, optional

1. Cook pasta according to package directions; drain.
2. Meanwhile, heat peas, green beans, carrots and tomatoes in separate
   large saucepan while pasta is cooking.
3. Mix in pasta and heat through. Season with salt and pepper, if desired.
   Garnish with Parmesan cheese, if desired.

Serves: 8   Serving size: ⅛ recipe

Variation

For a hearty main dish, add cooked chicken or ham.

NUTRITION FACTS PER SERVING

Calories	131	*Carbohydrate choices*	2
Carbohydrate	27 g		
Protein	5 g	*Exchanges*	1 starch
Fat	1 g		2 vegetable
Saturated fat	<1 g		
Fiber	3 g		
Sodium	355 mg		

Springtime Vegetable Pasta ☺

12 ounces fettuccine or other long pasta
1 bag (16 ounces) frozen Birds Eye® Farm Fresh Mixtures Cauliflower,
   Baby Whole Carrots and Snow Pea Pods
⅓ cup light creamy Caesar, Italian or ranch salad dressing
1 teaspoon dried basil
1 teaspoon garlic powder
⅓ cup grated Parmesan cheese
Salt and pepper to taste, optional

1. Cook pasta according to package directions; drain.
2. Cook vegetables according to package directions; drain.
3. Combine pasta, vegetables, dressing, basil and garlic powder in large skillet; mix well. Cook over medium heat just until heated through.
4. Add cheese; toss to coat pasta. Season with salt and pepper, if desired.

Serves: 8   Serving size: ⅛ recipe

NUTRITION FACTS PER SERVING

Calories	195	*Carbohydrate choices*	2
Carbohydrate	32 g		
Protein	8 g	*Exchanges*	2 starch
Fat	4 g		1 vegetable
Saturated fat	1 g		
Fiber	3 g		
Sodium	438 mg		

Hearty Pasta Italia ☺

1 green pepper, cut into strips
1 medium onion, halved, thinly sliced
1 clove garlic, minced
2 teaspoons vegetable oil
1 can (14½ ounces) Italian-style stewed tomatoes
1 jar (12 ounces) Heinz® Fat Free Mushroom Gravy
1 package (16 ounces) bow tie pasta, cooked and drained

1. In large skillet, sauté pepper, onion and garlic in oil until crisp-tender.
2. Drain tomatoes, reserving ⅓ cup liquid. Cut tomatoes into bite-sized pieces.
3. Add tomatoes, reserved liquid and gravy to vegetable mixture. Simmer 3 minutes.
4. Add pasta and toss to coat.

Serves: 10   Serving size: ¹/₁₀ recipe

NUTRITION FACTS PER SERVING

Calories	256	*Carbohydrate choices*	3
Carbohydrate	45 g		
Protein	7 g	*Exchanges*	3 starch
Fat	2 g		
Saturated fat	<1 g		
Fiber	2 g		
Sodium	519 mg		

Three Bean Salsa ☺

1 envelope Lipton® Recipe Secrets® Savory Herb with Garlic Soup Mix
½ cup water
1 large tomato, chopped
1 cup canned cannelini or red kidney beans, drained
1 cup canned black or pinto beans, drained
1 cup canned chickpeas or garbanzo beans, drained
2 teaspoons white or white wine vinegar, optional
Chopped fresh parsley or cilantro for garnish, optional

1. In 12-inch skillet, blend soup mix with water. Bring to a boil over high heat; stir in tomato. Reduce heat to low and simmer 3 minutes.
2. Stir in beans and simmer 3 minutes or until heated through.
3. Stir in vinegar, if desired. Garnish with parsley or cilantro, if desired.

Serves: 8   Serving size: ½ cup

Serving Suggestion

Serve as a side dish or topping with grilled poultry, beef, lamb or pork.

NUTRITION FACTS PER SERVING

Calories	114	*Carbohydrate choices*	1
Carbohydrate	20 g		
Protein	6 g	*Exchanges*	1 starch
Fat	1 g		1 very lean meat
Saturated fat	<1 g		
Fiber	5 g		
Sodium	652 mg		

Sweet 'N Spicy Onion Glaze ☉

1 envelope Lipton® Recipe Secrets® Onion Soup Mix
1 jar (20 ounces) apricot preserves
1 cup (8 ounces) Wish-Bone® Lite® Sweet'n Spicy French Dressing

1. In small bowl, blend all ingredients. Cover and refrigerate until flavors blend, 3 hours to overnight.
2. Use as a glaze or dipping sauce for chicken, spareribs, kabobs, hamburgers or frankfurters. Brush on during last half of cooking.
3. Glaze can be stored covered in refrigerator up to 2 weeks.

Serves: 20   Serving size: 2 tablespoons

NUTRITION FACTS PER SERVING

Calories	94	*Carbohydrate choices*	1½
Carbohydrate	22 g		
Protein	1 g	*Exchanges*	1½ fruit
Fat	1 g		
Saturated fat	<1 g		
Fiber	1 g		
Sodium	286 mg		

Desserts

Easy Peanut Butter Cookies

1 can (14 ounces) Eagle® Brand Sweetened Condensed Milk (not evaporated milk)
¾ to 1 cup peanut butter
1 egg
1 teaspoon vanilla extract
2 cups all-purpose baking mix
Granulated sugar

1. Preheat oven to 350° F. In large mixing bowl, beat milk, peanut butter, egg and vanilla until smooth. Add baking mix; mix well. Chill at least 1 hour.
2. Shape dough into 1-inch balls. Roll in sugar. Place 2 inches apart on ungreased baking sheets. Flatten with fork.
3. Bake 6 to 8 minutes or until *lightly* browned (do not overbake). Cool. Store tightly covered at room temperature.

Serves: 30   Serving size: 2 cookies

NUTRITION FACTS PER SERVING

Calories	132	*Carbohydrate choices*	1
Carbohydrate	16 g		
Protein	4 g	*Exchanges*	1 starch
Fat	6 g		1 fat
Saturated fat	2 g		
Fiber	<1 g		
Sodium	153 mg		

Rice Krispies Treats®

¼ *cup margarine*

1 package (10 ounces, about 40 marshmallows) regular marshmallows or 4 cups miniature marshmallows (use fresh marshmallows for best results)

6 cups Kellogg's® Rice Krispies® cereal

Vegetable cooking spray

Oven Directions

1. Melt margarine in large saucepan over low heat. Add marshmallows and stir until completely melted. Remove from heat.
2. Add cereal. Stir until well coated.
3. Using buttered spatula or waxed paper, press mixture evenly into 13 x 9 x 2-inch pan coated with cooking spray. Cut into squares when cool.

Microwave Directions

1. Microwave margarine and marshmallows on high 2 minutes in microwave-safe bowl. Stir to combine. Microwave on high 1 minute longer. Stir until smooth.
2. Add cereal. Stir until well coated.
3. Using buttered spatula or waxed paper, press mixture evenly into 13 x 9 x 2-inch pan coated with cooking spray. Cut into squares when cool.

Serves: 24   Serving size: 1 (2 x 2-inch) square

NUTRITION FACTS PER SERVING

Calories	82	*Carbohydrate choices*	1
Carbohydrate	16 g		
Protein	1 g	*Exchanges*	1 starch
Fat	2 g		
Saturated fat	<1 g		
Fiber	<1 g		
Sodium	104 mg		

Chocolate Banana Cupcakes

Vegetable cooking spray

1 package Betty Crocker® Sweet Rewards™ Reduced-Fat Devils Food Cake Mix

1½ cups (3 large) mashed ripe bananas

3 eggs

1 tub Betty Crocker® Sweet Rewards™ Reduced-Fat Ready-to-Spread Frosting (any flavor)

1. Preheat oven to 350° F. Place paper baking cups in 24 medium muffin cups or spray bottoms of cups with cooking spray.
2. Stir dry cake mix, bananas and eggs in large bowl, using spoon, until blended (about 50 strokes). Fill muffin cups about ⅔ full. (If necessary, refrigerate remaining batter while first pan bakes.)
3. Bake 15 to 20 minutes or until toothpick inserted in center comes out clean and top springs back when touched lightly in center. Remove from pan and completely cool on wire rack. Frost cupcakes.

Serves: 24   Serving size: 1 cupcake

NUTRITION FACTS PER SERVING

Calories	168	*Carbohydrate choices*	2
Carbohydrate	34 g		
Protein	2 g	*Exchanges*	2 starch
Fat	3 g		
Saturated fat	1 g		
Fiber	1 g		
Sodium	207 mg		

Glazed Carrot Raisin Cupcakes

1 package (18 ounces) spice cake mix
1 can (10¾ ounces) Campbell's® Healthy Request® Condensed Tomato
   Soup
½ cup water
2 eggs
½ cup shredded carrot
½ cup raisins
1 cup confectioners' sugar
3 tablespoons apple juice

1. Preheat oven to 350° F. Place paper baking cups in 24 medium muffin
   pan cups. Set aside.
2. Mix cake mix, soup, water and eggs according to cake mix package
   directions. Fold in carrot and raisins. Spoon batter into muffin cups,
   filling almost full.
3. Bake 20 minutes or until toothpick inserted in center comes out clean.
   Remove from pan and cool completely on wire rack.
4. Mix sugar and juice until smooth. Frost cupcakes.

Serves: 24   Serving size: 1 cupcake

NUTRITION FACTS PER SERVING

Calories	138	*Carbohydrate choices*	2
Carbohydrate	27 g		
Protein	2 g	*Exchanges*	1 starch
Fat	3 g		1 fruit
Saturated fat	1 g		
Fiber	<1 g		
Sodium	203 mg		

Traditional Pumpkin Pie

1 can (16 ounces, about 2 cups) pumpkin
1 can (14 ounces) Eagle® Brand Sweetened Condensed Milk
   (not evaporated milk)
2 eggs
1 teaspoon ground cinnamon
1/2 teaspoon ground ginger
1/2 teaspoon ground nutmeg
1/2 teaspoon salt
1 (9-inch) unbaked pastry shell

1. Preheat oven to 425° F. In large mixing bowl, combine all ingredients except pastry shell; mix well. Pour into pastry shell.
2. Bake 15 minutes. Reduce oven temperature to 350° F and bake 35 to 40 minutes longer or until knife inserted 1 inch from edge comes out clean. Cool. Refrigerate leftovers.

Serves: 8   Serving size: 1/8 pie

NUTRITION FACTS PER SERVING

Calories	399	*Carbohydrate choices* 3½	
Carbohydrate	53 g		
Protein	9 g	*Exchanges* 3½ starch	
Fat	17 g	3 fat	
Saturated fat	8 g		
Fiber	2 g		
Sodium	393 mg		

Cool 'N Easy™ Fruit Pie

²/₃ cup boiling water
1 package (4-serving size) Jell-O® Brand Gelatin Dessert, any flavor
¹/₂ cup cold water
Ice cubes
3¹/₂ cups Cool Whip® Lite Whipped Topping, thawed
1 cup fresh raspberries
1 9-inch graham cracker crumb crust, baked

1. In large bowl, stir boiling water into gelatin 2 minutes or until dissolved.
2. Mix cold water and enough ice cubes to make 1¹/₄ cups. Add to gelatin, stirring until slightly thickened. Remove any unmelted ice.
3. Gently stir in whipped topping using wire whisk. Fold in fruit.
4. Refrigerate until mixture is very thick and will mound. Spoon into pie crust. Refrigerate 2 hours. Garnish with additional fruit.

Serves: 8   Serving size: 1 slice (¹/₈ pie)

Variations

In place of the raspberries, try 1 cup fresh blueberries, halved pitted dark sweet cherries or chopped peeled fresh peaches, apricots or pears; ¹/₂ cup *each* sliced banana, chopped pear and halved seedless grapes; 1 can (8³/₄ ounces) apricots, sliced peaches or pear halves, drained and chopped; 1 can (20 ounces) crushed pineapple in juice, drained; or 1 can (8³/₄ ounces) fruit cocktail, drained.

NUTRITION FACTS PER SERVING

Calories	267	*Carbohydrate choices*	2¹/₂
Carbohydrate	35 g		
Protein	2 g	*Exchanges*	1¹/₂ starch
Fat	14 g		1 fruit
Saturated fat	7 g		2 fat
Fiber	1 g		
Sodium	135 mg		

Strawberry Lime Dessert

2 cups boiling water, divided
1 package (4-serving size) Jell-O® Brand Lime Flavor Gelatin Dessert
½ cup cold water
1 container (8 ounces) Breyer's® Plain or Vanilla Lowfat Yogurt
1 package (4-serving size) Jell-O® Brand Strawberry Flavor Gelatin
* Dessert*
1 package (10 ounces) frozen strawberries in light syrup

1. In medium bowl, stir 1 cup of the boiling water into lime gelatin
   2 minutes or until completely dissolved. Stir in cold water. Refrigerate
   about 45 minutes or until slightly thickened (consistency of unbeaten
   egg whites).
2. Stir in yogurt with wire whisk until smooth. Pour into 2-quart serving
   bowl. Refrigerate about 15 minutes or until set but not firm (should
   stick to finger when touched and should mound).
3. In medium bowl, stir remaining 1 cup boiling water into strawberry
   gelatin 2 minutes or until completely dissolved.
4. Stir in frozen berries until separated and gelatin is thickened (spoon
   drawn through leaves definite impression).
5. Spoon berry mixture over lime gelatin mixture. Refrigerate 2 hours or
   until firm. Serve. Store leftover dessert in refrigerator.

Serves: 10   Serving size: ½ cup

NUTRITION FACTS PER SERVING

Calories	106	*Carbohydrate choices*	1½
Carbohydrate	24 g		
Protein	3 g	*Exchanges*	1½ fruit
Fat	<1 g		
Saturated fat	<1 g		
Fiber	1 g		
Sodium	60 mg		

New-fashioned Vanilla Custard

1 package (3.4 ounces) instant vanilla pudding and pie filling mix
1 cup skim milk
1 cup Land O Lakes® Light Sour Cream
1 cup low-fat vanilla flavored yogurt
1 cup fresh strawberries, raspberries, blueberries or blackberries

1. Place instant pudding mix in medium bowl. With wire whisk, stir in milk until mixture is smooth and slightly thickened.
2. Add sour cream and yogurt; whisk until smooth. Cover; refrigerate at least 1 hour.
3. Spoon custard into 6 individual dessert dishes; top with assorted berries.

Serves: 6   Serving size: ⅙ recipe

Tip

One (0.9 ounce) package sugar-free instant vanilla pudding and pie filling mix may be substituted.

NUTRITION FACTS PER SERVING

Calories	176	*Carbohydrate choices*	2
Carbohydrate	32 g		
Protein	6 g	*Exchanges*	2 starch
Fat	3 g		
Saturated fat	2 g		
Fiber	1 g		
Sodium	317 mg		

Lemon Berry Crunch Parfaits ⊙

1 tub (8 ounces) Cool Whip® Lite Whipped Topping, thawed
2 containers (8 ounces each) lemon low-fat yogurt
2 cups blueberries
2 cups low-fat granola cereal

1. In large bowl, fold whipped topping into yogurt with wire whisk until smooth.
2. Layer whipped topping mixture, blueberries and cereal alternately in 10 (6-ounce) dessert glasses.
3. Refrigerate until ready to serve.

Serves: 10   Serving size: 1 6-ounce glass

NUTRITION FACTS PER SERVING

Calories	176	*Carbohydrate choices*	2
Carbohydrate	31 g		
Protein	4 g	*Exchanges*	2 starch
Fat	4 g		
Saturated fat	3 g		
Fiber	2 g		
Sodium	87 mg		

Ever-So-Easy Fruitcake

3 eggs, slightly beaten
1 can (14 ounces) sweetened condensed milk
1 jar (27 ounces) mincemeat
2 cups mixed candied fruit
1 cup coarsely chopped nuts
2 cups Kellogg's® Corn Flake Crumbs
1 teaspoon baking soda
Vegetable cooking spray

1. Preheat oven to 300° F. In large mixing bowl, combine eggs, milk, mincemeat, fruit and nuts. Mix well.
2. Add corn flake crumbs and baking soda; blend well. Pour batter into 9-inch tube pan or Bundt pan coated with cooking spray.
3. Bake 2 hours until wooden toothpick inserted near center comes out clean. Cool in pan for 5 minutes. Remove from pan. Cool on wire rack.

Serves: 16   Serving size: 1 slice

NUTRITION FACTS PER SERVING

Calories	388	*Carbohydrate choices* 5
Carbohydrate	71 g	
Protein	6 g	*Exchanges* 1 starch
Fat	10 g	4 fruit
Saturated fat	3 g	2 fat
Fiber	1 g	
Sodium	435 mg	

Baked Apple Puffs

5 Buena Vida™ Fat Free Flour Tortillas
1 can apple pie filling
1 teaspoon ground cinnamon
¼ cup seedless raisins
Vegetable cooking spray
½ cup powdered sugar
1 tablespoon skim milk

1. Remove tortillas from refrigerator. Let stand at room temperature for 15 to 30 minutes. Preheat oven to 375° F. Mix together pie filling, cinnamon and raisins. Evenly divide filling onto the middle of the 5 tortillas.
2. Fold both sides of tortilla toward the middle to keep filling from spilling out; fold bottom half of tortilla up and top half down to close. Repeat for all tortillas.
3. Place tortillas seam side down on baking sheet sprayed lightly with cooking spray. Spray top and sides of tortillas lightly with cooking spray. Bake for 8 to 10 minutes or until light golden brown.
4. In small bowl, mix together powdered sugar and milk. Drizzle over baked tortillas.

Serves: 5   Serving size: 1 puff

NUTRITION FACTS PER SERVING

Calories	260	*Carbohydrate choices*	4
Carbohydrate	59 g		
Protein	2 g	*Exchanges*	1 starch
Fat	2 g		3 fruit
Saturated fat	<1 g		
Fiber	2 g		
Sodium	172 mg		

Sour Cream Cherry Cobbler

Vegetable cooking spray
1²/₃ cups all-purpose baking mix
²/₃ cup sugar
²/₃ cup Land O Lakes® Light Sour Cream
¹/₃ cup skim milk
¹/₄ teaspoon almond extract
1 can (21 ounces) cherry pie filling
¹/₄ cup sliced almonds
1 tablespoon sugar

1. Preheat oven to 375° F. Spray 9-inch square pan with cooking spray. In medium bowl, combine baking mix, sugar, sour cream, milk and almond extract. Stir together until smooth.
2. Spread batter in pan; spoon pie filling evenly over batter.
3. Bake 35 to 40 minutes or until golden. Mix almonds and sugar; sprinkle over cobbler.
4. Return cobbler to oven and continue baking 10 to 20 minutes or until toothpick inserted in center comes out clean. Cut into 8 squares.

Serves: 8   Serving size: 1 square

NUTRITION FACTS PER SERVING

Calories	305	*Carbohydrate choices*	4
Carbohydrate	58 g		
Protein	4 g	*Exchanges*	2 starch
Fat	7 g		2 fruit
Saturated fat	2 g		2 fat
Fiber	2 g		
Sodium	353 mg		

Apple Crisp

6 large apples (about 8 cups), cored, peeled and sliced
1/3 cup firmly packed brown sugar
1/3 cup flour
1/2 teaspoon ground cinnamon
2 tablespoons margarine or butter
1 cup Post® Grape-Nuts Flakes or Post® Bran Flakes, lightly crushed

1. Preheat oven to 375° F. Arrange apple slices in 8-inch square baking
   pan.
2. Mix sugar, flour and cinnamon in large bowl. Cut margarine into flour
   mixture until mixture resembles fine crumbs. Stir in cereal.
3. Sprinkle flour mixture over apples. Bake 30 to 35 minutes or until
   apples are tender. Serve warm.

Serves: 8   Serving size: 1/8 recipe

NUTRITION FACTS PER SERVING

Calories	157	*Carbohydrate choices* 2	
Carbohydrate	33 g		
Protein	1 g	*Exchanges*	1 starch
Fat	3 g		1 fruit
Saturated fat	1 g		
Fiber	3 g		
Sodium	74 mg		

Cool Raspberry Fruit Dip ◷

½ cup Seven Seas® Free Raspberry Vinaigrette Fat Free Dressing
⅓ cup Breyer's® Lowfat Vanilla Yogurt
¾ cup Cool Whip® Lite Whipped Topping, thawed
Fresh-cut fruit

1. Mix dressing, yogurt and whipped topping until smooth. Refrigerate.
2. Serve with fruit for dipping.

Serves: 8   Serving size: 2 tablespoons

NUTRITION FACTS PER SERVING

Calories	30	*Carbohydrate choices*	0
Carbohydrate	5 g		
Protein	1 g	*Exchanges*	Free
Fat	1 g		
Saturated fat	1 g		
Fiber	0 g		
Sodium	211 mg		

Breakfasts

Breakfast Yogurt ☺

$^1/_2$ cup nonfat vanilla yogurt
2 tablespoons wheat germ
Pinch of cinnamon
2 strawberries, sliced
$^1/_2$ small banana, sliced
1 tablespoon Post® Grape Nuts cereal

1. Stir ingredients together in small serving bowl.
2. Serve immediately.

Serves: 1   Serving size: 1$^1/_4$ cup

NUTRITION FACTS PER SERVING

Calories	212	*Carbohydrate choices* 3	
Carbohydrate	41 g		
Protein	10 g	*Exchanges*	1 starch
Fat	2 g		1 fruit
Saturated fat	1 g		$^1/_2$ milk
Fiber	4 g		
Sodium	94 mg		

Cinnamon Streusel Coffee Cake

Vegetable cooking spray
⅓ cup firmly packed brown sugar
½ teaspoon cinnamon
1¾ cups Bisquick® Reduced Fat Baking Mix
¾ cup skim milk
¼ cup granulated sugar
1 tablespoon margarine, melted
1 egg

1. Preheat oven to 375° F. Spray a 9-inch round pan with cooking spray. Mix brown sugar and cinnamon until crumbly; set aside.
2. Stir remaining ingredients until blended. Spread in pan; sprinkle with brown sugar mix.
3. Bake 18 to 23 minutes or until golden brown.

Serves: 10   Serving size: 1 slice

NUTRITION FACTS PER SERVING

Calories	149	*Carbohydrate choices*	2
Carbohydrate	28 g		
Protein	3 g	*Exchanges*	2 starch
Fat	3 g		
Saturated fat	1 g		
Fiber	<1 g		
Sodium	275 mg		

Breakfast Quesadillas ⏱

1 cup shredded reduced-fat Monterey Jack cheese
1 cup shredded reduced-fat cheddar cheese
$^1/_2$ cup diced cooked ham
$^1/_3$ cup chopped and seeded tomatoes
$^1/_4$ cup chopped green onion
4 Azteca® Flour Tortillas

1. Preheat oven to 375° F. Combine shredded cheeses in bowl; set aside.
   Separately, combine ham, tomatoes and green onion.
2. Heat tortillas according to package directions. Divide both cheese and
   ham mixtures into fourths and place on top half of each tortilla. Fold
   bottom half of each tortilla over filling, forming a half moon. Place on a
   lightly greased baking sheet.
3. Bake 6 to 8 minutes or until edges of tortillas are light golden brown
   and cheese is melted.

Serves: 4   Serving size: $^1/_4$ recipe

NUTRITION FACTS PER SERVING

Calories	270	Carbohydrate choices	1
Carbohydrate	16 g		
Protein	22 g	Exchanges	1 starch
Fat	13 g		3 meat
Saturated fat	7 g		
Fiber	1 g		
Sodium	665 mg		

Breakfast Vegetable Stir-fry with Rice ☺

2 tablespoons vegetable oil
1 bag (16 ounces) Flav-R-Pac® Vegetable Stir-Fry with Rice®
4 ounces pre-cooked sliced ham, turkey or Canadian bacon cut into strips
8 eggs, lightly beaten
1 cup shredded reduced-fat cheddar or Monterey Jack cheese

1. Heat oil in wok or large skillet over medium heat.
2. Add frozen vegetables and rice and stir-fry about 4 minutes.
3. Add ham and beaten eggs; cook, stirring, until eggs are firm.
4. To serve, top with shredded cheese and place in microwave for about
   30 seconds or under broiler just until cheese is melted.

Serves: 6   Serving size: ⅙ recipe

NUTRITION FACTS PER SERVING

Calories	257		*Carbohydrate choices*	1
Carbohydrate	11 g			
Protein	19 g		*Exchanges*	1 starch
Fat	15 g			2 meat
Saturated fat	5 g			1 fat
Fiber	4 g			
Sodium	482 mg			

Frittata with Artichokes ☺

1 envelope Lipton® Recipe Secrets® Savory Herb with Garlic Soup Mix
8 eggs
¾ cup skim milk
1 teaspoon margarine or butter
1 cup (about 4 ounces) artichoke hearts, canned in water, diced and
   drained

1. In medium bowl, blend soup mix, eggs and milk; set aside.
2. In omelet pan or 8-inch nonstick skillet, melt margarine over low heat and cook egg mixture, lifting set edges with spatula and tilting pan to allow uncooked mixture to flow to bottom.
3. When bottom is set, top with artichokes. Reduce heat to low and cook, covered, 3 minutes or until eggs are completely set. Cut into 4 wedges.

Serves: 4   Serving size: 1 wedge

Variations

Substitute Lipton® Recipe Secrets® Golden Herb with Lemon or Golden Onion Soup Mix for Savory Herb and Garlic Soup Mix.

NUTRITION FACTS PER SERVING

Calories	205	*Carbohydrate choices*	1
Carbohydrate	13 g		
Protein	15 g	*Exchanges*	1 starch
Fat	11 g		2 meat
Saturated fat	3 g		
Fiber	3 g		
Sodium	751 mg		

Sausage and Eggs Brunch Casserole

Vegetable cooking spray
1 package (14 ounces) The Turkey Store® Breakfast Sausage Patties
1½ cups fat-free egg substitute
¼ to ½ teaspoon black pepper
⅔ cup chopped red pepper
⅔ cup chopped green pepper
⅔ cup chopped onion

1. Preheat oven to 325° F. Spray 9 x 9-inch baking dish and large skillet with cooking spray.
2. Heat skillet over medium-high heat about 30 seconds. Add sausage patties. Cook 12 to 15 minutes or until lightly browned and no longer pink in center, turning occasionally. Drain. Place in baking dish.
3. Stir black pepper into egg substitute. Pour mixture over patties. Bake 20 to 25 minutes or until firm but still moist.
4. Meanwhile, wipe skillet with paper towel. Spray again with cooking spray. Heat over medium-high heat about 30 seconds. Add peppers and onion. Cook and stir 3 to 5 minutes or until tender.
5. To serve, cut sausage and egg mixture into squares and top with cooked peppers and onions.

Serves: 6   Serving size: ⅙ recipe

NUTRITION FACTS PER SERVING

Calories	166	*Carbohydrate choices*	0
Carbohydrate	4 g		
Protein	20 g	*Exchanges*	3 lean meat
Fat	7 g		
Saturated fat	2 g		
Fiber	1 g		
Sodium	729 mg		

Broccoli and Sausage Quiche

Vegetable cooking spray
1 package (14 ounces) The Turkey Store® Breakfast Sausage Links
2 cans (8 ounces each) refrigerated crescent rolls
1 package (16 ounces) frozen chopped broccoli, cooked and drained
1 jar (2 ounces) diced pimiento, drained
$\frac{1}{2}$ cup shredded reduced-fat cheddar cheese
$1\frac{1}{2}$ cups egg substitute
1 cup skim milk
1 tablespoon flour
1 teaspoon Worcestershire sauce
$\frac{1}{4}$ teaspoon onion powder
$\frac{1}{4}$ teaspoon garlic powder
$\frac{1}{8}$ teaspoon black pepper

1. Preheat oven to 400° F. Spray large skillet with cooking spray; heat over medium-high heat about 30 seconds. Add sausage links. Cook 12 to 15 minutes or until lightly browned and no longer pink in center, turning occasionally. Remove from skillet; cool slightly. Cut each link into 4 pieces.
2. Separate crescent dough into 4 long rectangles. Place rectangles in ungreased 15 x 10 x 1-inch baking pan. Press over bottom and up sides to form crust. Seal perforations. Bake 6 minutes. Remove from oven.
3. Sprinkle crust evenly with broccoli, sausage pieces, pimiento and cheese.
4. In medium bowl, combine egg substitute and remaining ingredients; mix well. Pour egg mixture evenly over broccoli mixture.
5. Bake 25 to 28 minutes or until center is set and crust is deep golden brown. Let stand 5 to 10 minutes. Cut into 20 pieces.

Serves: 10   Serving size: 2 pieces

NUTRITION FACTS PER SERVING

Calories	290	*Carbohydrate choices*	2
Carbohydrate	27 g		
Protein	19 g	*Exchanges*	1½ starch
Fat	12 g		1 vegetable
Saturated fat	4 g		2 meat
Fiber	2 g		
Sodium	1040 mg		

Denver Bacon Burrito ◑

2 slices Louis Rich® Turkey Bacon
2 (7-inch) flour tortillas
¼ red or green pepper, chopped
1 tablespoon chopped onion
½ cup egg substitute
2 tablespoons Kraft® Shredded Reduced Fat Cheddar Cheese
Salt and pepper to taste, optional

1. Cook turkey bacon in small nonstick skillet on medium heat 5 minutes or until lightly browned. Place 1 turkey bacon slice on each tortilla.
2. Add pepper and onion to hot skillet; cook and stir 1 to 2 minutes.
3. Add egg substitute to vegetables; cook and stir 1 to 2 minutes or until set.
4. Divide egg mixture between tortillas; sprinkle with cheese. Season with salt and pepper, if desired. Fold tortillas over filling.

Serves: 2   Serving size: 1 burrito

Tip

To hold for serving, wrap filled burritos in foil and place in warm oven. Hold up to 30 minutes.

NUTRITION FACTS PER SERVING

Calories	187	*Carbohydrate choices*	1
Carbohydrate	20 g		
Protein	12 g	*Exchanges*	1 starch
Fat	6 g		1 meat
Saturated fat	2 g		
Fiber	2 g		
Sodium	482 mg		

Country Breakfast Casserole

1 tablespoon vegetable oil
1 bag (16 ounces) frozen O'Brien potatoes
1 container (12 ounces) Morningstar Farms® Scramblers
1 cup skim milk
2 tablespoons flour
4 ounces shredded reduced-fat cheddar cheese
¼ teaspoon black pepper
1 package (8 ounces) Morningstar Farms® Breakfast Links, chopped
Vegetable cooking spray

1. Preheat oven to 350° F. Heat oil in medium skillet. Fry potatoes in oil until golden.
2. Mix scramblers, milk, flour, cheese, pepper and links in mixing bowl. Fold into hot potato mixture.
3. Spray 8 x 12-inch baking dish with cooking spray. Pour mixture into baking dish. Bake 45 minutes.

Serves: 8   Serving size: ⅛ recipe

NUTRITION FACTS PER SERVING

Calories	308	*Carbohydrate choices*	2
Carbohydrate	30 g		
Protein	17 g	*Exchanges*	2 starch
Fat	14 g		2 meat
Saturated fat	4 g		
Fiber	3 g		
Sodium	925 mg		

Saturday Skillet Breakfast

12 slices Louis Rich® Turkey Bacon, cut into ½-inch pieces
1 medium potato, cut into small cubes
2 green onions, thinly sliced
½ teaspoon chili powder
1 carton (8 ounces) cholesterol-free egg substitute or 4 eggs, beaten

1. Place turkey bacon and potatoes in nonstick skillet. Cook on medium heat 12 minutes or until potatoes are fork-tender, stirring frequently.
2. Stir in onions and chili powder.
3. Pour egg substitute evenly over mixture; cover. Reduce heat to low and cook 5 minutes or until mixture is set. Cut into 4 wedges.

Serves: 4   Serving size: 1 wedge

NUTRITION FACTS PER SERVING

Calories	156	*Carbohydrate choices*	½
Carbohydrate	10 g		
Protein	13 g	*Exchanges*	½ starch
Fat	7 g		2 lean meat
Saturated fat	2 g		
Fiber	1 g		
Sodium	709 mg		

Beverages

Sher-bit Smoothie ⊙

¹⁄₂ medium ripe banana
¹⁄₂ cup orange sherbet
¹⁄₃ cup Minute Maid® Lemonade

1. Combine all ingredients in blender and blend until smooth and creamy.

Serves: 2   Serving size: ¹⁄₂ cup

NUTRITION FACTS PER SERVING

Calories	109	*Carbohydrate choices*	2
Carbohydrate	26 g		
Protein	1 g	*Exchanges*	2 fruit
Fat	1 g		
Saturated fat	1 g		
Fiber	1 g		
Sodium	24 mg		

Fruited Orange Shake ☽

2 cups Minute Maid® Pure Premium® Orange Juice
1 pint Dole® Raspberry or Pineapple Sorbet

1. Combine all ingredients in blender and blend until smooth and creamy.

Serves: 8   Serving size: ½ cup

NUTRITION FACTS PER SERVING

Calories 93   *Carbohydrate choices* 1½
Carbohydrate 23 g
Protein <1 g   *Exchanges*   1½ fruit
Fat 0 g
Saturated fat 0 g
Fiber <1 g
Sodium 12 mg

Orange Banana Slush ☉

1½ cups Minute Maid® Pure Premium® Orange Juice
1 large ripe banana, cut into chunks
1 tablespoon honey
1 to 2 teaspoons vanilla extract
1½ cups ice cubes

1. Combine all ingredients except ice in blender and blend until smooth and creamy.
2. Add ice and blend until thick. Serve in chilled glasses.

Serves: 4   Serving size: 1 cup

NUTRITION FACTS PER SERVING

Calories	91	*Carbohydrate choices*	1½
Carbohydrate	22 g		
Protein	1 g	*Exchanges*	1½ fruit
Fat	<1 g		
Saturated fat	0 g		
Fiber	1 g		
Sodium	2 mg		

Banana Chocolate Milkshake ◔

1 cup skim milk
2 tablespoons Hershey's® Cocoa
Granulated sugar substitute to equal ⅓ cup sugar
1 teaspoon vanilla extract
1 medium ripe banana, sliced
8 large ice cubes

1. Pour milk into blender. Add cocoa. Cover; blend on low speed until well mixed.
2. Add sugar substitute, vanilla extract and banana. Cover; blend until smooth and creamy.
3. Add ice cubes, one at a time, blending until thick. Serve immediately.

Serves: 2   Serving size: 1½ cup

NUTRITION FACTS PER SERVING

Calories	114	*Carbohydrate choices*	1½
Carbohydrate	22 g		
Protein	6 g	*Exchanges*	1 fruit
Fat	1 g		½ milk
Saturated fat	<1 g		
Fiber	3 g		
Sodium	65 mg		

Hot Cocoa Au Lait ☻

2 tablespoons Hershey's® European Style Cocoa or Hershey's® Cocoa
¼ cup hot water
1½ cups skim milk
Granulated sugar substitute to equal 8 teaspoons sugar
¼ teaspoon vanilla extract

1. In small saucepan, place cocoa; gradually stir in water. Cook over medium heat, stirring constantly, until mixture boils; boil and stir until smooth and hot, about 1 minute.
2. Immediately stir in milk; continue cooking and stirring until mixture is hot. Do not boil.
3. Remove from heat; stir in sugar substitute and vanilla extract. Serve immediately.

Serves: 2   Serving size: about 1 cup

NUTRITION FACTS PER SERVING

Calories	78	*Carbohydrate choices* 1
Carbohydrate	12 g	
Protein	7 g	*Exchanges* 1 milk
Fat	1 g	
Saturated fat	<1 g	
Fiber	2 g	
Sodium	96 mg	

Fast & Easy Banana Colada ◔

1 cup Old Home® Vanilla Nonfat Yogurt
1 frozen medium banana, peeled
½ cup crushed pineapple, packed in juice, undrained
½ teaspoon shredded coconut
2 ice cubes

1. Combine all ingredients in blender and blend until smooth and creamy.

Serves: about 3   Serving size: ¾ cup

Tip
Remove peeling from banana and wrap in plastic before placing in freezer.

NUTRITION FACTS PER SERVING

Calories	115	*Carbohydrate choices*	2
Carbohydrate	26 g		
Protein	4 g	*Exchanges*	1 fruit
Fat	<1 g		½ milk
Saturated fat	<1 g		
Fiber	1 g		
Sodium	36 mg		

Classic Fruit Punch ☉

½ cup Tang® Orange Flavor Drink Mix
4 cups water
1 package (10 ounces) frozen unsweetened strawberries, partially thawed
1 can (6 ounces) frozen concentrated lemonade
2 cups chilled club soda
Ice cubes

1. Place drink mix, water, strawberries and lemonade in punch bowl. Stir until drink mix is dissolved and strawberries are separated. Refrigerate.
2. Stir in club soda and ice cubes just before serving.

Serves: 16   Serving size: ½ cup

NUTRITION FACTS PER SERVING

Calories 49	*Carbohydrate choices* 1
Carbohydrate 12 g	
Protein <1 g	*Exchanges* 1 fruit
Fat 0 g	
Saturated fat 0 g	
Fiber 1 g	
Sodium 8 mg	

Berry Lemonade ⊙

6 cups cold water, divided
1 package (10 ounces) frozen unsweetened raspberries
1 tub Country Time® Lemonade Flavor Sugar Free Low Calorie Drink Mix

1. Place 3 cups of the water, raspberries and drink mix in blender; cover. Blend on high speed until smooth and creamy; strain mixture to remove seeds.
2. Pour into large plastic or glass pitcher. Stir in remaining 3 cups water. Refrigerate until ready to serve. Stir before serving.

Serves: 7   Serving size: 1 cup

Variations

For Strawberry Lemonade, substitute 1 package (10 ounces) frozen unsweetened strawberries for raspberries; do not strain mixture. For Raspberry Tropical Fruit Drink, substitute 1 tub Crystal Light Tropical Passions® Pineapple Orange Flavor Low Calorie Soft Drink for lemonade flavor drink mix.

NUTRITION FACTS PER SERVING

Calories	24	*Carbohydrate choices*	½
Carbohydrate	6 g		
Protein	<1 g	*Exchanges*	½ fruit
Fat	<1 g		
Saturated fat	0 g		
Fiber	3 g		
Sodium	0 mg		

Cranberry Lemonade Spritzer ⏱

1 tub Crystal Light® Lemonade or Pink Lemonade Flavor Low Calorie Soft Drink Mix
1 bottle (48 ounces) light cranberry juice cocktail
1 bottle (1 liter) chilled club soda
Ice cubes

1. Place drink mix in large plastic or glass pitcher. Add cranberry juice cocktail; stir to dissolve. Refrigerate.
2. Pour into large punch bowl just before serving. Stir in club soda and ice cubes.

Serves: 10   Serving size: 1 cup

NUTRITION FACTS PER SERVING

Calories	24	*Carbohydrate choices* ½	
Carbohydrate	6 g		
Protein	0 g	*Exchanges* ½ fruit	
Fat	0 g		
Saturated fat	0 g		
Fiber	0 g		
Sodium	30 mg		

Banana Punch ☉

4 cups cold water, divided
1 tub Crystal Light Tropical Passions® Strawberry Kiwi or Passionfruit
  Pineapple Flavor Low Calorie Soft Drink Mix
2 medium ripe bananas
1 bottle (1 liter) chilled club soda
Ice cubes

1. Place 1 cup of the water, drink mix and bananas in blender; cover. Blend on high speed until smooth and creamy. Pour into large plastic or glass pitcher.
2. Stir in remaining 3 cups water. Refrigerate until ready to serve. Just before serving, add club soda. Serve over ice.

Serves: 9   Serving size: 1 cup

NUTRITION FACTS PER SERVING

Calories	27	*Carbohydrate choices*	½
Carbohydrate	7 g		
Protein	<1 g	*Exchanges*	½ fruit
Fat	<1 g		
Saturated fat	0 g		
Fiber	1 g		
Sodium	24 mg		

Hot and Spicy Tomato Cocktail ☉

1 can (28 ounces) whole tomatoes
3 tablespoons lime juice
⅛ teaspoon cayenne pepper
2 tablespoons chopped fresh mint
4 lime slices for garnish, optional

1. Place tomatoes in blender and blend until smooth and creamy. Strain seeds.
2. Combine the pureed tomatoes, lime juice, cayenne pepper and mint in a non-aluminum saucepan.
3. Warm over low heat and simmer for 10 minutes. Garnish each serving with a lime slice, if desired, and serve hot.

Serves: 4   Serving size: about ¾ cup

NUTRITION FACTS PER SERVING

Calories	42	*Carbohydrate choices* ½	
Carbohydrate	9 g		
Protein	2 g	*Exchanges* 2 vegetable	
Fat	<1 g		
Saturated fat	0 g		
Fiber	2 g		
Sodium	326 mg		

Index

Books of Related Interest from
IDC Publishing

Convenience Food Facts
A Quick Guide for Choosing Healthy Brand-Name Foods in Every Aisle of the Supermarket

Fourth Edition

Arlene Monk, RD, LD, CDE
Nancy Cooper, RD, LD, CDE

Completely revised and expanded, *Convenience Food Facts* has everything you need to plan quick, healthy meals using packaged foods. This edition highlights low-fat choices among more than 3,000 popular brand-name products. Also includes carbohydrate choices and exchange values. Ideal for anyone using a meal-planning method to lose weight or to manage a health problem such as diabetes. $12.95; ISBN 1-885115-36-9

Fast Food Facts
Fifth Edition

Marion J. Franz, MS, RD, LD, CDE

The original book of facts on fast food, this new edition offers readers hard-to-find nutrition information, including carbohydrate choices, food exchanges, and designated good food choices. Recommended for anyone who frequents fast food restaurants.

Trade edition: $7.95; ISBN 1-885115-42-3

Pocket edition: $4.95; ISBN 1-885115-43-1

These books are available at your local bookstore.
Visit our website at www.idcpublishing.com